CHAOS TO CLARITY
THE TAO OF RISK MANAGEMENT

JOSEPH W. MAYO

PUBLISHING

Chaos to Clarity – The Tao of Risk Management
© 2009 by Joseph W. Mayo

Cover design by Brian Zuckerman
www.BrianZuckerman.com

Editing, book design and production by John Everett Button,
www.JohnEverettButton.com

Assistant editing and book design by Bethany Burger

Manuscript formatting and graphics by Julius Broqueza

Published by Milton Chadwick & Waters Publishing
5008 Shortgrass lane, Haymarket, VA, 20169
www.MiltonChadwickandWaters.com

For information, please contact J. W. Mayo Consulting, LLC.
13910 West Price Lake Rd, Box 655, Cable, WI 54821
www.jwmc-llc.com

Although the author and publisher have made every effort to ensure the accuracy and completeness of information contained in this book, we assume no responsibility for errors, inaccuracies, omissions, or any inconsistency herein. Any slights of people, places, or organizations are unintentional.

ATTENTION CORPORATIONS, UNIVERSITIES, COLLEGES, and PROFESSIONAL ORGANIZATIONS: Quantity discounts are available on bulk purchases of this book for educational, gift purposes, or as a premium for increasing magazine subscriptions or renewals. Special books or book excerpts can also be created to fit specific needs. For information, please contact JWMC, LLC, 13910 West Price Lake Rd, Box 655, Cable, WI 54821 or email at joseph.mayo@jwmc-llc.com.

First published by Milton Chadwick & Waters Publishing 4/1/2015

ISBN: 978-0-9884542-3-1(*e*)
ISBN:978-0-9884542-2-4 (*sc*)
ISBN: 978-0-9884542-1-7 (*hc*)

Library of Congress Control Number: 2015901239

PUBLISHING
Milton Chadwick & Waters Publishing
www.MiltonChadwickandWaters.com

Chaos to Clarity – The Tao of Risk Management
is dedicated to my wife Kathy
for her constant encouragement and
gentle prodding to "finish your book."

Acknowledgments

A big thank you to my colleagues who were excellent sounding boards and helped me formulate my position on risk management. A special thank you to Bret, Huba, Saul, Steven, Tareen, and Tony for reviewing manuscript drafts and providing valuable feedback. Lastly, I would like to thank my daughters Shawna, Brooklyn, Brittny, Andrea, Maddi, and Kinzy for their support and tireless promotion of Chaos to Clarity: The Tao of Risk Management. Thanks...

About The Author

Joseph W. Mayo is an Information Technology professional with over 20 years of experience. Mr. Mayo is a PMI certified Project Management Professional (PMP),Risk Management Professional (RMP),and a Certified Risk and Information Systems Control (CRISC) professional. Mr. Mayo has worked for a variety of professional services companies including Computer Sciences Corporation, Keane Incorporated, ManTech International, and NTT DATA. He is a frequent speaker and conference presenter on topics that include risk management, project management, and quality assurance. Career highlights include the following:

- Program Manager for project #7 of the top 100 IT Projects of 2006 by InfoWorld.
- Developed PMO procedures, the collaboration workspace, and Executive level dashboards for a PMO to divest a large International conglomerate ($18B 2005 revenue). The PMO was responsible for cloning 112 Corporate Applications for four separate operating companies and renegotiating 1,300 telecommunications, IT service and license contracts without impacting the day to day operations of any one of the operating companies.
- Developed a risk management maturity roadmap for the U.S. Customs and Border Protection (CBP) Office of Technology Innovation and Acquisition (OTIA) and was instrumental in the development and implementation of the Enterprise risk policy.

Table of Contents

PREFACE

I have been increasingly frustrated by ineffective risk management in the IT industry. My frustration was the driving force to write this book. *Chaos to Clarity: The Tao of Risk Management* is my attempt to bring clarity to the murky practice of risk management. Tao is commonly thought of as a series of principles to live by. The goal of *Chaos to Clarity* is to present basic risk management principles I have found to be highly effective over the years.

As a Quality Assurance Manager, I've conducted more than 60 project assessments since the late 1990s. During that time I was continually amazed by the endless failures of risk management in the IT industry. Project managers with comprehensive risk management training still had projects fail because of ineffective risk management.

I set out to improve risk management by creating a series of training courses. I based the risk training courses on a variety of risk management books and countless discussions with industry professionals.

After several years of training project managers and conducting project assessments on failed projects, I'm forced to conclude that the risk management processes touted by various professionals and standards organizations simply do not work. The risk management processes don't work because they are wrong; they don't work because there is insufficient guidance on how to apply the techniques and principles in the everyday life of project managers and other risk practitioners.

Risk management processes established by the Project Management Institute (PMI), the International Standards Organization (ISO) and the Australia – New Zealand (AS/NZS) standards organization are reasonable processes. However, three areas these standards organizations neglect are 1) how to properly identify risks, 2) how to objectively quantify risk impact, and 3) how to establish and maintain risk models so future projects can benefit from both the successes and failures of risk management.

I was recently inspired while reading a series of books and articles about prominent risk management failures. I was inspired not by the fact that risk management is broken, but by the fact that other authors and I independently arrived at similar conclusions. Douglas Hubbard, a world renown risk management expert, suggests that risk management could benefit from a more structured approach based on actuarial science, and by calibrating the probabilities of risk occurrence (Hubbard, 2009). I tend to agree with Hubbard, and I have espoused the need to objectively quantify both risk impact and probability for many years.

The balance of this book will present a risk management approach I developed based on industry standards and nearly three decades of slogging through the trenches as a Project Manager. The information contained in this book easily translates to nearly any industry and can be applied to many non-technical situations and environments. This standards-based approach provides the tools and techniques needed to properly identify risks and objectively quantify risk impact so risks can be effectively managed. *Chaos to Clarity* also includes processes required to deliver true value to individuals and organizations through effective risk management.

You may notice my liberal use of the term "effective." Over the past several decades I have seen many organizations that have extremely efficient risk management processes that do not translate to effective risk management. Efficient is defined as the ability to accomplish a job with a minimum expenditure of time and effort. Effective is defined as success in producing a desired result. The ability to effectively manage risk is far more important than minimizing the expenditure of time and effort of managing risk. Effectiveness is valued over efficiency because the most critical risks often have catastrophic effects if they occur, so the time and effort spent managing the risk pales in comparison to the impact of the risk. Standards bodies strive to drive efficiency into processes and expect efficiency will translate to effectiveness. Process efficiency does translate to effectiveness in cases where there is a finite set of variables and outcomes such as a manufacturing process. Risks have a nearly infinite set of variables making it very difficult to optimize the risk management process. Furthermore, a single risk can have catastrophic effects so a highly effective risk management process that reliably treats risks is far more valuable than a highly optimized process that may be untested or less reliable. An inefficient risk management process that is highly effective is much more valuable to an organization than an efficient risk management process that is highly ineffective; hence, the focus on effectiveness over efficiency.

INTRODUCTION

According to Ming-Dao (1996), there are eight qualities associated with Taoism: simplicity, flexibility, disciplined, sensitivity, independent, focused, cultivated, and joyous. Effective risk management aligns quite nicely with these qualities.

Three Taoist principles, simplicity, flexibility, and discipline are critical success factors for effective risk management, and you will see these concepts reiterated throughout the book. Many organizations and tools tend to complicate risk management by utilizing complex prioritization schemes, algorithms, and procedures. Conversely, organizations that focus on simplicity and risk management fundamentals tend to be very successful. There are no industry studies that demonstrate numerous prioritization levels is better than a basic High, Medium, Low prioritization scheme. It is important for risk practitioners to not rule anything out; flexibility is key. Risk practitioners must maintain an independent view so they can present decision makers with unbiased information and be prepared to alter their approach to meet the constantly changing environment. Taoism describes discipline as taking orderly actions toward specific goals without imposing a harsh structure. One of my primary objectives for this book is to present a disciplined approach combined with simplicity and flexibility to achieve effective risk management.

The remaining five Taoist principles sensitivity, independence, focused, cultivated, and joyous are equally important, but are extremely difficult to implement without implementing the three critical principles of simplicity, flexibility, and disciplined. In Taoism, sensitivity is the observation of others. Independence is the freedom to operate with few constraints.

Effective risk management requires people and organizations to take a broad view and evaluate risks from different perspectives—in essence, observations of others. A focused risk management approach is required to maximize benefits or advantages. Organizations can realize the Tao quality of "cultivated" when they strive to improve and continuously refine their risk management approach. Last but not least, applying these Taoist qualities will result in a joyous situation brought on by effective risk management!

High Reliability Organizations (HROs) exhibit many of these Taoist characteristics. The "high reliability organization" paradigm was developed by a group of researchers at the University of California, Berkeley, to capture common operational aspects among aircraft carriers, commercial aviation, and nuclear power (Sutcliffe, 2011). Sutcliffe suggests that HROs organize in ways that increase the quality of attention across the organization, thereby enhancing people's alertness and awareness to details (e.g. observation of others and focused). Sutcliffe goes on to state that alertness and awareness allow people and organizations to detect subtle ways in which contexts vary and to call for contingent responses. This alertness and awareness culture forms a basis for individuals to interact continuously as they develop, refine and update a shared understanding of the situation they face and for their ability to act on that understanding (e.g. cultivated and flexible).

Chaos to Clarity is divided into three parts. Part I sets the stage by providing some history of risk management, establishing context and presenting key concepts used throughout the book. Part I also discusses four risk management challenges project managers frequently encounter.

Part II presents a risk management process I developed over the past ten years. The process described in Part II is a hybrid process composed of elements from five industry standards (ISO 16085, ISO 31000, AN/NZS 4360, ISACA's Risk IT, and the PMBOK) and my own experience over the past three decades.

Part III presents tips, tools, techniques, and case studies to help improve the effectiveness of individual and organizational risk management capability.

I use some examples from the IT industry to illustrate key points but the information contained in this book is not specific to any one industry. *Chaos to Clarity* is not intended to be an academic discussion of risk management. It is a guide for individuals to improve the effectiveness of their risk management process and practices. *Chaos to Clarity* strives to align with the eight Taoist principles with special emphasis on simplicity, flexibility, and discipline.

PART I

HISTORY
AND
CONTEXT

CHAPTER ONE

A Working Definition

There are seven key risk management concepts that must be thoroughly understood and communicated to stakeholders. The key risk management concepts are as follows:

- The definition of risk,

- Risk theory,

- Risks versus issues,

- Types of risks,

- Risk management versus risk mitigation,

- Risks versus opportunities, and

- Known-unknowns versus unknown-unknowns.

These key concepts wreak havoc on risk management if they are misunderstood or improperly communicated, so it is extremely important to have a clear understanding of them. However, a basic understanding of these key concepts is sufficient; there is no need to be an expert in them.

There are as many definitions of risk as there are risk references. This chapter will present a unified definition of risk based on three industry sources. According to Merriam-Webster OnLine Search (n.d.), risk is defined as "someone or something that creates or suggests a hazard." Australia-New Zealand AS/NZS-4360 and International Standards Organization (ISO)ISO 31000 *Risk Management -- Guidelines on Principles and Implementation of Risk Management* define risk as "the chance of something happening that will have an impact on objectives" (Joint Standards Australia/Standards New Zealand Committee OB-007, 2004). The Project Management Body of Knowledge (PMBOK) defines project risk as "an uncertain event or condition that, if it occurs, has a positive or negative effect on at least one project objective, such as time, cost, scope or quality" (Project Management Institute, 2008, p. 275).The unified definition of risk that will be used throughout this book is

> *An uncertain event that, if it occurs, will have a negative effect on one or more objectives.*

History of Risk Theory

Risk practitioners need not be mathematicians or statisticians, but they must recognize there are tools, techniques, and processes that can be borrowed from the insurance and financial service industries to improve risk management in other industries. This book is a practical guide and does not contain academic or theoretical discussions of risk theory or probability. *Chaos to Clarity* does present interesting tidbits from time to time that readers may find interesting and choose to explore further.

Risk theory and the study of probability are not recent phenomena; they have been around for more than 400 years. Risk theory began in the 1500's with a treatise written by Girolamo Cardan and entitled *DeLudo Aleae* (Book on Games of Chance). Cardan was a renowned Italian medical doctor and instructor in Mathematics who wrote his treatise in 1550, although it was not published until 1663. Cardan was an avid gambler and his treatise presented some ideas of basic probability applied to games of chance using dice. Cardan's treatise is the first historical record of probability theory (Leung, n d.). A variety of works on probability (many focused on games of chance) were published in the 1600's and 1700's by a series of notable authors including Johannes Kepler, Galilei Galileo, Rene Descartes, Pier de Fermat, Blaise Pascal, Christiaan Huygens, and others.

Actuarial science is a discipline that applies mathematics and statistics to assess risk in the insurance and finance industries. The roots of actuarial science can be traced back to a published work by Edmond Halley of Halley's Comet fame. Halley published a work in 1693 entitled *An Estimate of the Degrees of the Mortality of Mankind, Drawn from Curious Tables of the Births and Funerals at the City of Breslaw; With an Attempt to Ascertain the Price of Annuities upon Lives* (Halley, 1693). Halley's work included a "life table" which became the basis for computing life insurance premiums.

The role of actuarial science in risk management will become clear as we explore risk management challenges and shortcomings of currently accepted risk management processes. Keep in mind that the study of probability has spanned over 400 years so there are many lessons learned from a variety of industries that can be used for improving risk management practices. Actuarial science is a disciplined approach based on mathematics and has been around for over 300 years. Many lessons from the study of probability and actuarial science can, and should, be applied to risk management.

Risks vs Issues

It is extremely important for risk practitioners, stakeholders, and project teams to clearly understand the difference between risks and issues. A risk is something that has not yet occurred but, if it does, it will have a negative impact on one or more objectives. An issue, on the other hand, is something that is currently impacting one or more objectives.

Issues are frequently confused with risks causing significant challenges for risk management practitioners. Confusing issues and risks leads to ineffective risk management because precious risk management resources are wasted resolving issues instead of preventing risks, which, in turn, destines the project team to incur nearly every risk. Expending risk management time, money, and effort to resolve issues causes stake holders to question the project team's ability to effectively manage risk; once this happens many organizations simply stop managing risks because it appears to be a waste of time, money and effort.

Confusion arises when a risk is realized and the project doesn't close the risk and open an issue. As risks are realized it is imperative that the risk is closed, a new issue is opened, and both the issue and risk are cross-referenced. This technique may seem trivial but if this discipline is not enforced, the risk register quickly deteriorates into a hodgepodge of issues and risks resulting in confusion amongst external stakeholders. Once this happens, risk practitioners begin spending as much time clarifying and defending the risk register as they do actually managing risks. Confusion is further compounded by the fact that some risks that are realized may also continue to be a risk. Consider the following risk statement:"If a hurricane makes landfall, then the project schedule will be delayed by two months." If a hurricane does make landfall, then this risk will have been realized. If the landfall occurs early in the hurricane season, then it is reasonable to expect that it could occur again. Therefore, this risk could spawn multiple instances and should still be carried as an ongoing risk.

Most risks, on the other hand, are onetime events such as: "If a second data architect is not available at the start of the data model deliverable, then completion of the data model will be delayed by two months." This risk is cut and dried. If there are not two data architects available when the data model is scheduled to begin, then the risk is realized. The lack of data architect resources becomes an issue unless, of course, the risk has been effectively treated so as not to impact the schedule.

When a risk is realized or is imminent, the risk owner must decide whether the risk event is a onetime event or if recurrence is possible. If the risk is considered a onetime event, the owner should open an issue that references the risk, update the risk register to reference the newly opened issue, and close the risk. If there is potential for multiple occurrences of the risk, then the risk register must be updated to include all issues that are associated realization of the risk. The bi-directional cross references will prove to be extremely valuable when developing risk models. Risk models are discussed in more detail in Chapter Three.

Types of Risks

Primary Risks

Risk practitioners must manage three types of risks: primary risks, residual risks, and secondary risks. In industry and in this book, the term "risk" in used to generically reference all types of risk. The term "primary risk" is used to refer to a specific risk that can be documented and quantified. Primary risks are usually the only risks that are identified on a consistent basis; very few organizations actively manage residual and secondary risks.

Residual Risks

Residual risks are risks that remain after risk responses have been implemented (Project Management Institute, 2008, p.438). Your automobile insurance deductible is one example of a residual risk. Buying auto insurance transfers the owner's financial risk to the insurance company, but there is a residual risk from this transaction in the form of the collision deductible. There is an important lesson here for organizations that use subcontracting to transfer their risk. Transferring risk can be an effective strategy to reduce risk, but transferring risk does not eliminate all the risk.

Secondary Risks

Secondary risks are risks that arise as a direct result of implementing a risk response (Project Management Institute, 2008, p. 441). The Deepwater Horizon disaster provides an excellent example of a secondary risk. The primary risk faced by British Petroleum (BP) was damage to shorelines, beaches, and wildlife. BP's risk response to this primary risk was to apply chemical compounds called "dispersants" to the oil floating on the surface of the water (Lustgarten, 2010). These dispersants cause oil on the surface to breakup and sink to the bottom. However, the dispersants contain highly toxic chemicals that can kill fish and damage aquatic ecosystems. In implementing their risk response to the primary risk of shoreline damage, BP created a secondary risk of damage to the aquatic ecosystem.

Risk Management vs Risk Mitigation/Treatment

A significant impediment to effective risk management is the misguided perception that all risks must be mitigated. Effective risk management applies the appropriate amount of resources (e.g. effort and dollars) to each risk. The appropriate amount of resources may in fact be none. Effective risk management utilizes all four of the industry accepted risk treatment strategies. The four accepted treatment strategies are avoid, transfer, mitigate, and accept. Many organizations develop risk management plans that only refer to "risk mitigation." Effective risk management requires the discipline to evaluate all four risk management strategies, select a strategy, document risk treatment plans, and aggressively monitor risk treatment effectiveness.

A risk register is used to catalog risks. Risk registers must include all risks, not just risks that require mitigation. Risks in the risk register must be prioritized, and treatment plans must be developed for high priority risks, including those risks that are transferred, accepted, or avoided. Treatment plans for transferred and avoided risks are generally one-time activities, although they should be reviewed periodically to confirm that residual or secondary risks have not arisen. Effective treatment plans for accepted and mitigated risks require active management and oversight.

Risk vs Opportunity

Many risk management articles and texts present risk management and opportunity management as similar to one another. The PMBOK defines opportunity as "a condition or situation favorable to the project, a positive set of circumstances, a positive set of events, a risk that will have a positive impact on project objectives, or a possibility for positive changes" (Project Management Institute, 2008, pg. 431).

Many organizations tend to combine risk, issue and opportunity, (RIO) management. The combination of RIO tends to causes mass confusion. I agree that opportunities should be managed and leveraged to their fullest extent. However, I also believe sufficient differences exist between opportunity management and risk management such that each warrants separate treatment. Therefore, opportunity management is considered out of scope for this text. The focus of *Chaos to Clarity* is risk management without regard to opportunities. There is clearly a close relationship between issues and risks, but to avoid confusion, I have omitted lengthy discussions about issue management as the PMBOK and other industry models address issue management at length.

Known-Unknowns versus Unknown-Unknowns

The concept of known-known, known-unknowns and unknown-unknowns is an aspect of decision theory that plays a very important role in effective risk management. According to Wideman (1992), an Internationally recognized project management expert, a "known" is an item or situation containing no uncertainty. Therefore, a known-known refers to a situation or circumstance that is fully expected to occur.

A known-unknown refers to circumstances or outcomes that are known to be possible, but it is unknown whether or not they will be realized. For example, an organization may require deployments to be approved by a specific individual who is often unavailable. This is a classic case where a history of delays exists but less than 100% of the deployments are delayed, hence a known-unknown.

An unknown-unknown refers to circumstances or outcomes that were not conceived of by an observer at a given point in time (Answers.com, n.d.).

Known-unknowns are risks that can be reasonably expected to impact a given project, although the degree of impact and probability of occurrence cannot be immediately determined. Known-unknown are variables used to help to determine the amount of contingency reserve. The total impact of the known-unknowns should be used to determine the size of the contingency reserve. The size of the contingency reserve should be in terms of both budget and schedule.

An unknown-unknown is also referred to as a Black Swan event. Black Swan theory is based on Nassim Nicholas Taleb's article *The Black Swan: The Impact of the Highly Improbable* describing extreme events that cannot be reasonably conceived to happen (Taleb, 2007). Black Swan events are very rare occurrences that have far reaching impact. The plague that ravaged Medieval Europe, 9/11, the 2004 Indonesian Tsunami, and the Deepwater Horizon disaster are examples of Black Swan events. Unknown-unknowns or Black Swan events are nearly impossible to plan for because the probability, frequency, and impact simply cannot be estimated.

Risk Exposure

Risk exposure is the total impact risks have on an organization and is typically represented by four categories: schedule, budget, quality, or mission. Each individual risk represents some amount of schedule, budget, quality, or mission risk. The sum total of all individual risk exposure amounts represent the total organizational risk exposure that must be considered when making risk strategy decisions. Risk exposure is an important element used to establish an organization's risk tolerance and risk appetite. The organization's risk policy should establish risk exposure thresholds the organization can tolerate and effectively manage.

> *Management reserve is a risk management technique used to manage the impact of unknown-unknowns.*

Risk Tolerance

Risk tolerance is the level of risk exposure an organization or individual is willing to absorb. There is a close relationship between risk exposure, risk tolerance, and reserves. Reserve budgets are the total amount of reserve resources (e.g. budget, time, assets) an organization is prepared to reserve specifically for managing risk. Risk exposure is the cost of risk treatment plus any residual risk.

Consider the case where someone purchases a car for $30,000. The risk exposure is $30,000. People have varying degrees of risk tolerance and many of them will likely transfer this $30,000 risk by purchasing auto insurance. Transferring 100% of the risk is often quite costly; so many people agree to pay a deductible in exchange for lower insurance premiums.

The deductible indicates a person's risk tolerance. For example, Joe has a low risk tolerance and chooses a $250 deductible for his auto insurance. Bob, on the other hand, has a higher risk tolerance and chooses a $2,000 deductible. Let's assume Joe's insurance premiums are $140 per month and Bob's premiums are $80 per month. With no risk treatment, Joe and Bob's risk exposure is $30,000. Transferring the risk to an insurance company reduces Joe's risk from $30,000 to $1,930 ($140 monthly premium X 12 months + $250 deductible) and reduces Bob's risk from $30,000 to $2,960 ($80 monthly premium X 12 months + $2,000 deductible).

Now let's add reserves to the picture. Joe has a low risk tolerance so he would likely maintain a contingency reserve of $1,930, which is the total amount needed to pay premiums and the deductible. Bob has a higher risk tolerance and chooses to maintain a $2,000 contingency reserve, which is enough to pay the premiums and a portion of his deductible. At this point Joe's risk exposure is $0 and Bob's risk exposure is $960 ($2,960 risk exposure - $2,000 contingency reserve).

These examples are rather simplistic but serve to illustrate the relationships between risk exposure, risk tolerance and reserves. Actual risk scenarios are much more complex than the example above, but they still follow the same principles. The key is to understand the relationships between risk exposure, risk tolerance, and reserves. Revisit risk exposure, risk tolerance, and reserves anytime environmental or market conditions require a change to any one element.

CHAPTER TWO

Evolution of IT Risk Management

The evolution of modern day IT risk management began with the Project Management Institute (PMI) publishing the first edition of the Project Management Body of Knowledge (PMBOK) in 1987. While the PMBOK has changed significantly since 1987, the risk management elements have remaining relatively unchanged. As an active member of PMI and frequent volunteer for PMI workshops, I constantly strive to improve PMI's approach to risk management. Unfortunately, PMI lags behind the international risk management standards community. Other international organizations such as ISO and ISACA have significantly expanded risk management practices into governance and improvement.

Figure 1 shows the evolution of risk management over the past couple of decades and maps three risk management standards against the first edition of the PMBOK: Australia-New Zealand AS/NZS-4360, ISO/IEC 16085 Systems and software engineering – Life cycle processes – Risk Management, and ISACA's Risk IT. As you can see in the diagram, there have been a number of improvements in risk

	GOVERNANCE	RISK ANALYSIS	RISK TREATMENT	IMPROVEMENT
1987 PMBOK	• Risk Management Planning	• Risk Identification • Qualitative Analysis • Quantitative Analysis	• Risk Response Planning	
2004 AN/NZS 4360	• Communicate & Consult • Establish Context	• Identify Risks • Analyze Risks • Evaluate Risks	• Treat Risks • Monitor & Review Risks	
2006 ISO 16085	• Plan & Implement Risk Management • Manage the Project Risk Profile	• Risk Analysis	• Treat Risks • Monitor & Review Risks	• Evaluate Risk Management Process
2009 RISK IT	• Define Risk Universe & Scope Risk Management • Risk Appetite & Tolerance • Risk Awareness, Communication & Reporting	• Expressing & Describing Risk • Risk Scenarios	• Risk Response & Prioritization	• Risk Awareness, Communication & Reporting

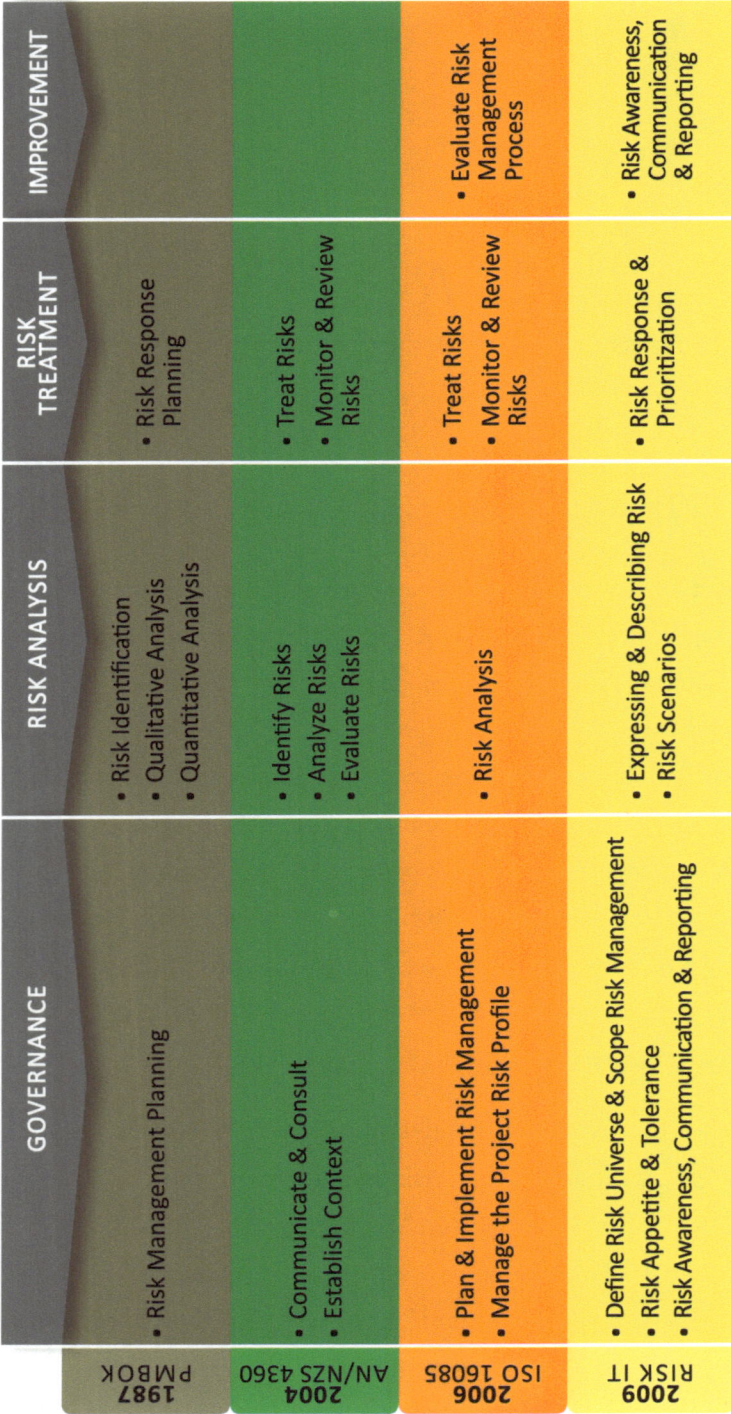

Figure 1 - Evolution of Risk Management

management standards and industry best practices since 2004 mainly in the area of governance.

The first major improvement to IT risk management came with the introduction of AN/NZS 4360 in 2004. AN/NZS 4360 aligned very closely with the PMBOK risk analysis processes but expanded the governance and risk treatment aspects of risk management. ISO 16085 followed two years later and borrowed heavily from AS/NZS 4360. ISO 16085 expanded risk management governance even further and introduced a portion of the standard dedicated to risk management process improvement. A number of significant changes to risk management came along in 2009 with the release of ISACA's Risk IT framework and practice guide.

Risk IT was a revolutionary change to IT risk management that significantly expanded the governance aspects of risk management, suggested that improvement activities begin in the governance and definition phase, introduced the concept of risk scenarios, and presented a simplified risk prioritization scheme. I have come to admire Risk IT's simplified prioritization scheme because it drives organizations to focus on risks with the greatest impact. The governance aspect of Risk IT include the same features of the other standards but places a very high degree of emphasis on defining the organization's risk appetite, risk tolerance, and risk universe.

I have come to rely almost exclusively on risk scenarios as a way to describe risks, because they more clearly describe the risk impact, and people seem to be able to grasp the scenarios better than they can individual risks. Risk IT applies to many areas other than IT, which is another reason why I leverage it quite extensively. Much work is being done in Great Britain with risk scenarios very similar to those described in Risk IT. A good example of a non-IT risk scenario can be found on the Warwickshire County Council website (http://www.warwickshire.gov.uk/communityriskregister)

The Warwickshire community defined nine risk scenarios, including industrial accidents, transport accidents, industrial technical failure, etc. Each risk scenario includes a number of risk events that could occur as part of the scenario, the impact to the community, the likelihood of occurrence, etc. Risk scenarios are discussed more fully in Chapter Six.

CHAPTER THREE

Risk Management Strategies

There are four accepted risk management strategies: accept, avoid, transfer, mitigate. It is critical that the risk management process includes a conscious decision to select a specific risk management strategy. I regularly encounter organizations that believe all risks must be mitigated and any risk that is transferred, avoided, or accepted is completely ignored, which is a recipe for disaster. Risks that are accepted, transferred, or avoided frequently result in secondary or residual risks. Therefore, regardless of the risk management strategy, it is imperative that all risks are added to the risk register and managed throughout the life of the project. Risk strategies are generally selected while prioritizing risks and are heavily influenced by the risk policy. For example, an organization with an appetite for risk and a willingness to tolerate a high degree of risk will likely accept a number of risks, whereas an organization that has a low risk tolerance will look to transfer or avoid most risks.

Transfer

Risk transfer is a strategy where risk is transferred to a third party. Two common ways to transfer risk are subcontracting and buying insurance. Risk practitioners should not be fooled into thinking that risks transferred to a third party are fully treated. The four steps to effectively treat transferred risks are 1) decide to transfer a risk, 2) document the risk in the risk register, 3) identify secondary risks 4) identify residual risks. Simply transferring the risk doesn't mean it has been effectively treated; transferring a risk may reduce the risk but it must still be monitored and managed.

Buying auto or homeowners insurance is a very simple example of risk transfer where residual risk is left over from the transfer in the form of a deductible. Another example where a risk is transferred would be by subcontracting the development of a critical software module to a third party. Subcontracting the critical software module does not guarantee that the software module will function as required or even be delivered on time. Subcontracting typically does reduce the risk to some degree but does not fully eliminate the risk.

Avoidance

Avoidance is a risk management strategy that seeks to circumvent the risk. For example, someone who seeks to avoid hurricane damage to a new house would build the house outside of the known hurricane zone(s), possibly in a non-coastal state. To avoid a project risk, an organization could simply cancel or de-scope the requirement(s) associated with the risk. There are clearly substantial costs associated with risk avoidance not to mention potential lost opportunities. Risk avoidance is typically found in highly conservative, risk averse organizations. Risk avoidance can be quite costly so it is important to take this factor into account when planning for risk management. Many organizations are sensitive to the fact that they are risk averse, and the organizational culture tends to shy away from formally documenting risks that they choose to avoid. To effectively manage risks in a risk averse organization, it is important to confirm that the risk policy accurately reflects the risk sensitivity of both the organization and key stakeholders so that realistic treatment plans can be developed.

Acceptance

Acceptance is a risk management strategy where a conscious decision is made to accept the risk. Acceptance is commonly used where the impact of the risk is projected to be less than the cost to treat and manage the risk. Factoring the impact of accepted risks into the contingency reserve is the most effective way to manage the overall impact to the project. A common risk management problem is that accepted risks are rarely documented in the risk register.

Risks are rarely static and their probability of occurrence and impact are likely to change over time. If an accepted risk changes to the extent that it requires treatment, the risk is often ignored because it has been "accepted" and consequently not documented. Accepted risks must be documented in the risk register and continually reviewed to confirm that the probability and impact has not changed. Accepted risks are also a subset of the known-known risks.

Mitigate

Mitigation is a risk strategy where a risk treatment plan is prepared. A risk treatment plan is based on a mitigation strategy or series of actions that will reduce the impact of the risk to some degree. A frequent problem with risk policies or risk management plans is that they are often based on the false assumption that all risks must be mitigated. It is unreasonable to expect that all risks can be mitigated and, as previously mentioned, it may not be cost effective to mitigate risks. The key to effective risk management is to recognize that risks must be managed and treated but not necessarily mitigated. Risk treatment plans will typically include a variety of risk management strategies, some of which will be risk mitigation.

CHAPTER FOUR

Risk Budgets

Three risk budgets must be considered during the risk management process: the project budget, contingency reserve budget, and management reserve budget. The project budget includes everything needed to deliver the project deliverables. The contingency reserve budget is used for treating risks that can be reasonably conceived or are known to have occurred on similar projects (e.g. known-unknowns). The management reserve budget is used for treating unknown-unknowns and invoking contingency plans. The contingency reserve should include resource and schedule allocations as well as budget dollars. Ultimately everything comes down to budget dollars, but some internal organizations find it easier to allocate internal resources based on effort and external resources based on budget dollars. Either way the key is to reserve the effort, calendar time, and/or budget in advance. The contingency reserve budget includes funds and resources used for all risk treatment strategies.

Most people and organizations are familiar with the contingency reserve budget. However, few organizations formally reserve funds and resources for this purpose, which is one reason risk management activities are difficult to quantify. The contingency reserve budget is used to manage all risks, including secondary risks and residual risks. The contingency reserve budget is often confused with the Management Reserve Budget, but the two reserve budgets have completely different purposes and should be kept separate and distinct. The management reserve budget is used to manage the effects of unknown-unknowns or Black Swan events. The amount of management reserve is based on the criticality of the project and the impact of project failure to the organization's mission.

A decision tree is a good tool for establishing the total risk exposure and contingency reserve. Decision trees are used to document risks that have many variables and multiple outcomes. Decision trees are used to objectively quantify risk impact so decision makers can make fact-based decisions and minimize the influence of opinions and emotions. Expected monetary value (EMV) is one outcome of a decision tree can be used to establish the contingency reserve budget. EMV is a derived value based on the cost of all conditions, potential return of all conditions, and the probability of occurrence for all conditions. The sum of the highest cost from each branch of a decision tree equals the total risk exposure, which is then used to establish the amount of contingency reserve. Contingency reserve budgets are based on an organization's risk tolerance and risk appetite. A risk-averse organization may reserve budget and effort amounts nearly equal to their total risk exposure, whereas a risk tolerant organization may allocate a small fraction of their total risk exposure.

Approval authority is one of the key differences between the various risk budgets. The Senior Management is typically authorized to allocate funds from the contingency reserve budget. The project sponsor generally authorizes the use of management reserve funds, but some organizations may require higher levels of approval.

Budgets Elements

Proper utilization of project budgets is one of the keys to successful risk management. A project budget consists of at least three elements: project budget, management reserve, and contingency reserve. Fixed price projects contain a fourth element which is often referred to as the risk premium. Some organizations bundle the risk premium with the management reserve; but combining these elements is problematic, making it very difficult for project managers to access the risk premium.

Effective risk management requires all stakeholders to understand 1) the project budget elements, 2) how the budgets are applied to risk management activities, and 3) what the approval process is for distributing budget funds.

Budget Element	Owner
Risk Premium	} Project Sponsor
Management Reserve	
Contingency Reserve	} Senior Management
Project Budget	} Project Manager

Figure 2 - Budget Elements

Some organizations will combine all budget elements into a single budget. Combining budget elements often leads to disastrous results overtime because stakeholders have no insight into whether budget overruns are the result of poor planning, poor executions, or poor risk management. Segregating the different budget elements provides greater transparency for stakeholders and helps facilitate continuous improvement.

Risk Premium

The risk premium is an additional amount that many organizations add to fixed price projects to account for unknown-unknowns and

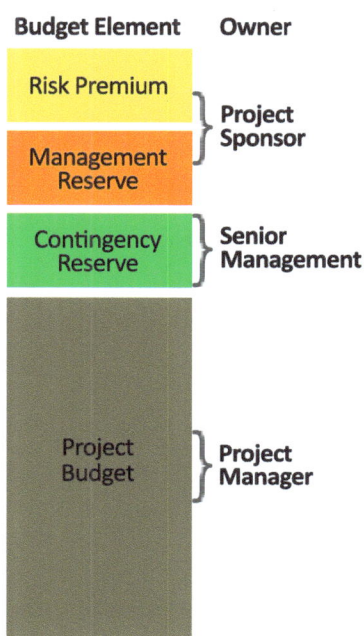

to make them comfortable enough to take on 100% of the risk. It is not unusual for risk premiums to be 30% - 50% of the estimated cost. Risk premiums can be significantly higher for one-time, high risk projects. Risk premiums should be used to offset unknowns such as changing market factors that make components more expensive, inaccurate estimates, unexpected expedite fees, higher shipping costs, etc.

Combining the risk premium with the management reserve makes it difficult for project managers to access needed funds. This is because the "risk" doesn't rise to the level of a Black Swan event, which is the primary reason for having a management reserve.

Management Reserve

The Management Reserve is used to manage the impact of Black Swan events (aka unknown-unknowns). An organization's risk tolerance and risk appetite will dictate the amount of budget dollars and personnel effort allocated to the management reserve. An organization with a high risk tolerance and a high appetite for risk will likely allocate little to no resources to managing the management reserve, whereas an organization with a low risk tolerance and/or appetite will likely allocate resources to manage the management reserve.

Contingency Reserve

The contingency reserve budget consists of budget dollars and personnel effort used to manage all risks, including secondary risks and residual risks (aka known-unknowns). Organizations with a Chief Risk Officer (CRO) or Office of Risk Management (ORM) are generally accountable for the contingency reserve. The Program / Project Management Office (PMO) is generally responsible for managing the contingency reserve process, which typically includes a risk review board to review and approve risks, budgets, etc. (see Governance and Oversight)

All risk strategies require some amount of effort and funds to implement. Even risks that are accepted can require money and effort to treat. Consider the following scenario:

> *A project identifies a schedule risk that delays the project completion by two weeks. Missing the project completion date results in a $5,000 penalty. The cost to compress the schedule is $7,500, so the stakeholders choose to accept the risk and pay the $5,000 penalty if the schedule date is missed.*

The $5,000 penalty should be included in the contingency budget.

Project Budget

The project budget is the estimated cost to complete the project. The project budget includes labor, materials, fees, and taxes. Some project managers inflate or pad estimates to account for known-unknowns. However, inflating or padding estimates is a bad practice as it tends to foster scope creep and tends to obscure estimating and risk management problems. Formally establishing a contingency reserve and a governance process to access the contingency reserve funds is a much more effective approach because it highlights the effectiveness of the estimating and risk management processes. Padding can obscure estimating and risk management problems until it is too late to take corrective action, at which time the Project Manager must begin tapping into the management reserve. Depending on where the project is in the life cycle, the impact could range from minor, if the project is near completion, to catastrophic if the project is before the halfway point.

Budget Management

Budget management is part of the overall risk governance process (see Governance and Oversight) and is tightly coupled with the risk review board (RRB) process. Risk management funds are released through the RRB process. Risks that have been identified and logged in the risk register are submitted to the RRB for consideration. The RRB adjudicates risks and releases risk treatment funds accordingly. Project schedule and budget baselines are updated after risk treatments funds are released by the RRB. Risk status reporting is typically defined in the RMP.

Time & Materials and Cost Reimbursable Projects

A Contingency Reserve Budget and a Management Reserve Budget must be formally established at the beginning of the project and reviewed at regular intervals throughout the life of the project. Budget distribution procedures and approval authorities must also be established in order to eliminate confusion and costly delays later in the project.

There are typically three approval authorities on most projects: Project Manager, Senior Management, and Project Sponsor. The Project Manager is responsible for managing the project budget and has the authority to request funds from either the Contingency Reserve or the Management Reserve. Senior Management is generally responsible for managing the Contingency Reserve Budget, which includes funds to manage known risks that have been identified and logged in the risk register. Senior Management is generally a single individual but can be a committee of Senior Managers in cases where the Contingency Reserve is very large. The Project Sponsor is generally the approval authority for the Management Reserve Budget, which includes funds that are applied to unknown risks that have not been contemplated by the stakeholders. Management Reserve funds are also used to reduce the impact of Black Swan events, although one should not expect the Management Reserve to be sufficient to fully mitigate the effects of a Black Swan event.

Converting assumptions to risk statements is an effective technique for identifying the risk premium and management reserve budgets.

CHAPTER FIVE

Common Risk Management Challenges

This chapter presents three strategic risk management challenges and two tactical risk management challenges. Strategic challenges are those that typically require organizational involvement to resolve, such as a Program Management Office (PMO), Risk Management Office (RMO), or Enterprise. Tactical challenges can generally be resolved by individuals at the project level. Together these five challenges are significant impediments to effective project risk management. These risk management challenges, if properly addressed, will minimize distraction and wasted effort as well as maximize the effective use of limited resources.

Organizational Challenges

Organizational Challenge # 1 – Risk Identification. I often see project teams scrambling around trying to manage all the risks in their risk registers. One of the fundamental problems with this approach is that most entries in the risk register are not actually risks at all but issues, conditions, symptoms, events and opinions.

I facilitated a risk assessment for a large ($1 billion +) government program. The initial list of "risks" included countless issues, conditions, symptoms, concerns, and opinions along with a few risks. More than

83% of the original risk register entries were eliminated during the risk analysis phase because they were symptoms, issues, concerns, opinions, etc. This characteristic is very typical of most risk registers where 15% - 20% of the risks in the register are actually risks.

The most common risk management challenge by far is the improper identification of risks. Improper identification of risks leads to wasted time, money, and effort. Demoralization of the risk management team because of their perceived inability to effectively manage risks is only one of the negative outcomes resulting from improper risk identification. The risk management team is often attempting to treat conditions, symptoms, events, and / or opinions that are indications a risk exists, but they are not actually treating the risk. The key point here is that the condition, symptom, etc. must be decomposed to the point that the actual risk is identified. I often review risk registers that contain literally dozens of supposed risks. However, the "risks" are actually symptoms or indications that a risk is present. For example, low employee satisfaction or loss of key personnel may listed as risks but these are likely symptoms most likely associated with a schedule risk. Improperly identified risks are nearly impossible to mitigate and end up wasting precious risk management resources.

According to Martin (2005), there are three types of risks that should be addressed in the risk plan: scope, schedule and cost. Process mature organizations that have an effective risk management record should further decompose project scope into quality and mission accomplishment risks. Risk management for most organizations is represented by a maximum of four context elements: schedule, budget, quality, and mission accomplishment. Chapter Nine describes risk identification techniques and processes in more detail

Organizational Challenge #2 – Disciplined Approach. There are generally a small number of risks that represent the vast majority of the total risk exposure for an organization. The frantic scrambling approach noted above causes organizations to lose sight of the total risk exposure, and they end up wasting precious resources on risks that have minimal impact on the organization's objectives. One of the critical success factors in risk management is to properly identify risks and then manage the risks that represent the greatest impact to the project. Organizations often find that the top three to five risks represent more than 50% of their total risk exposure, so focusing risk management efforts on those critical few risks will likely result in greater success.

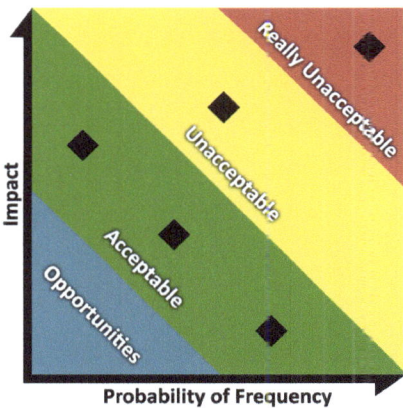

Figure 3 - Risk IT Risk Priority

I strongly advocate Control Objectives for Information and Related Technology (COBIT) and Risk IT approach to risk prioritization because they fully embrace the simplicity principle of Tao. COBIT is a governance framework that helps enterprises create value from IT by maintaining a balance between benefits, risk optimization, and resource use. Governing and managing IT in a holistic manner for the entire enterprise is one of the key tenants of COBIT. Risk IT is a companion to COBIT that focuses specifically on risk. Risk IT initially separates risks into two categories: acceptable risks and unacceptable risks. Acceptable risks are further categorized as acceptable risks or opportunities, and unacceptable risks are further categorized as unacceptable risks and really unacceptable risks. The Risk IT approach to prioritizing risks drives people and organizations to focus on the risks that have the greatest overall impact on organizational mission or project objectives. Otherwise, countless hours could be spent trying to decide which one of more than two dozen priority boxes the risk should be assigned to.

Organizational Challenge #3 – Risk Models. Documenting the effectiveness of the risk treatment plan or strategy may not necessarily impact the current project, but it will certainly affect later projects. A risk model is one method for documenting organizational risk management effectiveness. Risk models contain the risk that was treated, the treatment strategy, treatment plans that proved effective, and treatment plans that proved to be ineffective. What doesn't work is just as important as what does work, so make sure risk models contain both elements.

Risk model validation requires empirical data to be collected over time in order to establish a reasonable sample size so trends can be identified and proven. An effective outreach program must be established in order to communicate effective risk models throughout the organization. Risk models are only as good as the communication mechanism; high quality risk models without an effective communication mechanism are as good as no model at all.

Project Challenges

Project Challenge #1 – Risk Quantification. I see risks logs that list the impact as "major," "significant," "substantial," etc. There is no universally accepted definition of "significant" so one person's "significant"- may seem trivial to others. Without objectively quantifying risk impact there is no way for an organization to understand their total risk exposure and whether they are within the risk tolerance levels established by the organizational risk policy. To effectively mitigate a risk, its impact to the project must be objectively quantified so that treatment activities can be measured. It makes no sense to spend $50,000 to treat a risk that represents $10,000 in budget impact. Examples of objective quantification include three-week schedule delay, $50,000 budget overrun, 500 hours of rework, etc. Objective risk quantification is a frequent topic of debate with pundits stating the uncertainty of risk makes it impossible to objectively quantify. However, Case Study #2 in Chapter Sixteen clearly demonstrates that objective risk quantification is not only possible, but is critical to the risk treatment process.

Risk scoring and risk normalization are variations of risk quantification that are quite problematic in my opinion. The risk scoring and normalization schemes I have seen tend to be very complex. Complex schemes not only violate the simplicity principle of Tao but are also very difficult to modify as the organization or market conditions change. Risk scores tend to bury the true risk impact which, caused organizations to waste limited risk management resources by treating risks that will have minimal impact on the overall project outcome or organizational objectives.

I conducted a risk assessment for a large government agency and found they normalized risks using a concept called a Risk Adjusted Cost (RAC). Using the RAC calculation, a risk with a $225,000 budget impact and a "High" probability of occurrence yields the same RAC as a risk with a $175,000 budget impact and a "Very High" probability of impact. The RAC of these two risks are equal. However, there is a $50,000 difference in the estimated impact. In this case the RAC would cause these two risks to be treated equally when, in fact, the $175,000 risk should receive prompt attention because the probability of occurrence is much higher than the $225,000 risk.

Findings and research from the Deepwater Horizon disaster also support the fact that normalization, or the desire to simplify interpretations, has a negative impact on an organization's ability to effectively manage risk. Simplifying interpretations is troublesome because it gives people a false sense of exactly what they face, limits the kinds of precautions taken, and severely limits the number of undesired consequences people can imagine (Sutcliffe, 2011).

Project Challenge # 2 – Effective Treatment Plans. A risk or series of risks with a single treatment action is one indication that the project risk has not been properly identified. Further analysis often reveals that the same action is assigned to a variety of risks—another indication that the true risk has not yet been properly identified. More often than not, a risk will require multiple actions to be effectively managed. Risk scenario is an excellent tool that can help develop highly effective treatment plans.

Insist on proper risk identification, drive objective quantification of risk impact, build actionable risk treatment plans, and document the results of all risk management activities.

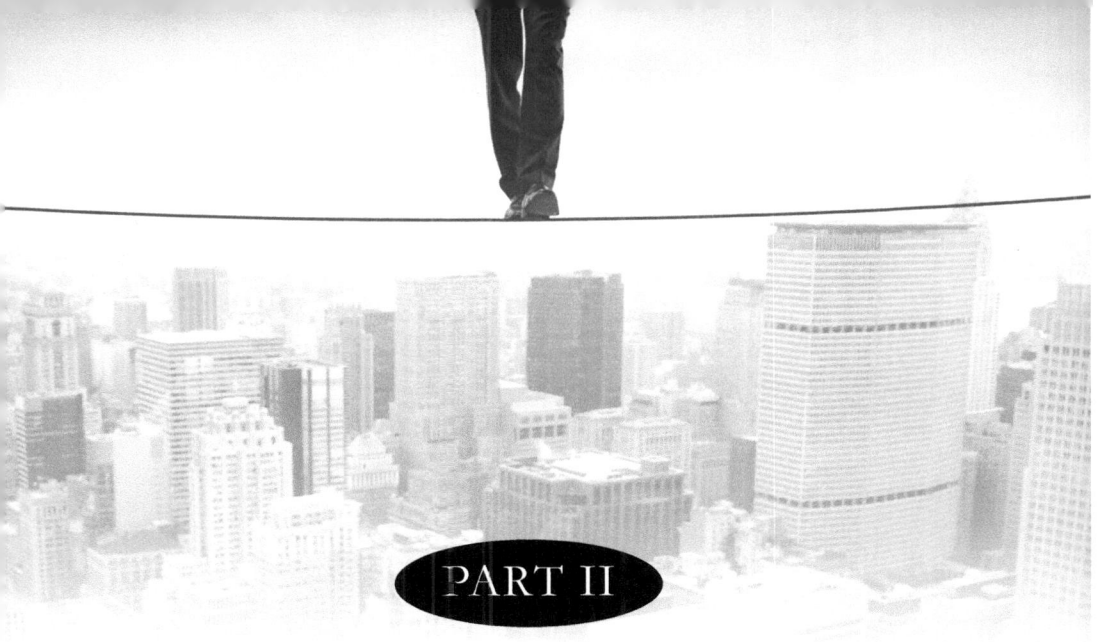

PART II

ELEMENTS

OF

RISK

MANAGEMENT

CHAPTER SIX

A Standards Based Approach

There are a number of risk management standards, including PMI's Project Management Body of Knowledge (PMBOK), Australia-New Zealand AS/NZS-4360, International Standards Organization (ISO) ISO 31000 Risk Management -- Guidelines on Principles and Implementation of Risk Management, ISO/IEC 16085 Systems and software engineering – Life cycle processes – Risk Management, National Institute of Standards and Technology (NIST) 800-30 Risk Management Guide for Information Technology Systems, Factor Analysis of Information Risk (FAIR), Institute of Electrical and Electronics Engineers (IEEE) 1540, and many others. PMBOK, AS/NZS-4360, and ISO/IEC 16085 focus primarily on project risk management, whereas NIST 800-30, ISO 31000 and FAIR have a much broader scope and focus primarily on organizational or Enterprise risk management. Fundamentally, all of these standards have five basic components in common: risk management planning, risk identification, risk analysis, risk treatment, and risk monitoring.

The nebulous nature of risk makes it difficult to effectively manage the risk. However, aligning with the Taoist principles creates an environment that brings structure and discipline to the risk management process. A disciplined process with emphasis on simplicity and flexibility yields a highly effective process that is dynamic and can quickly adapt to changing market conditions. An effective risk management program includes both a strategic and a tactical component. The strategic component of risk management begins with a set of risk management principles that includes management acknowledgment and support, recognition that risk management is an inexact science, and recognition that a disciplined approach yields significant value to the organization.

The single most important organizational principle is management acknowledgment and support of risk management. Management acknowledgment and support is characterized by organizational processes that make risk management integral to operational processes, especially the decision making process. Management must also recognize that acknowledgment and support includes a high degree of transparency and involves decision makers from all levels of the organization.

Risk management is an inexact science that explicitly addresses uncertainty. Organizations must recognize that risk management is based on limited and incomplete data. Therefore, an effective risk management program should strive to exhibit HRO characteristics and be dynamic, iterative, responsive to change, and designed for tailoring based on market situations, organizational changes, and organizational process maturity. Because of the uncertainty associated with risks, an organization must be willing to make risk-based decisions using available information and not wait until all risk factors are known.

> *Failure to acknowledge and support making risk-based decisions with limited information dooms an organization to incur nearly every risk they identify.*

Another key principle is recognition that, even though risk management is an inexact science, the risk management process must be disciplined and systematic. A disciplined and systematic risk management program facilitates continual improvement and creates value for the organization. It is important for an organization to recognize that human and cultural factors can either facilitate or hinder meeting organizational objectives. It is imperative that cultural factors are taken into account when developing and executing a risk management program.

The Strategic Process

A defined risk policy is the first and most important component of the strategic process. A formal risk policy describes the organization's tolerance for risk, sets thresholds for risk tolerance and appetite, defines the roles and responsibilities of Senior Management, provides a high level description of the risk management process, and provides guidance on the use of risk budgets. The risk policy sets the overall direction for risk management, but it does not contain the details required to implement the policy.

Risk policy is implemented using risk management plans and risk review boards. Risk management plans contain the day-to-day operational steps needed to effectively manage risks. Risk review boards are used to verify and validate compliance with the risk policy and assure risks are being properly managed. Four excellent references for the strategic aspects of risk management are ISO 31000, ISO/IEC 15026, Risk IT, and ISO/IEC 16085.

The Tactical Process

An effective tactical risk management process consists of nine components, six discrete process steps and three oversight activities. The six process steps are: establish risk contexts, identify risks, quantify impact, prioritize, treat, and monitor treatment. The three oversight activities span the entire risk management process to ensure compliance, foster development of risk models, and facilitate a feedback loop to leverage lessons learned and best practices.

Four references for the tactical aspects of risk management are Risk IT, PMBOK, AS/NZS-4360, and ISO/IEC 16085. These four references include the same basic nine components, although they may be ordered and grouped differently (see Figure 1). The process described in this chapter is a hybrid process I developed based on Taoist principles and nearly 30 years of experience in the IT industry. The hybrid process is fundamentally based on the PMBOK, AS/NZS-4360, ISO/IEC 16085, and ISACA's Risk IT.

Some may argue that the sequence is less important than the actual process. However, the sequence depicted in Figure 4 is what I have found most effective, as it maximizes risk management resources by focusing on high impact risks and reduces the amount of time, effort, and money wasted on low impact risks.

Figure 4 - Risk Management Process

CHAPTER SEVEN

Governance and Oversight

The project risk management process is not complex, but executing the process can be very difficult. In order for project risk management to be effective, the process must be enforced at both the tactical and strategic level. Effective oversight of the tactical risk management process can be provided by a combination of Quality Assurance reviews and Management reviews. Oversight of the strategic risk management process requires an effective governance process consisting of a risk policy, risk management plans, and a risk review board. Without adequate oversight, the effectiveness of organizational risk management can quickly deteriorate due in large part to the challenging nature of project risk management.

While management consists of actual decisions made, governance offers a structure for making those decisions. It is critical for organizations to establish a governance structure so executive sponsors can steer the organization as necessary, and the more tactical business and technical personnel can continue with the day to day development of effective results.

The role of governance is to offer a decision-making mechanism that consists of policy-makers, committees, and review boards. An executive steering committee (ESC) typically focuses on strategy, investment and architecture. The ESC also has responsibility to assign the decision-making authority and accountability. Compliance monitoring provides oversight to assure policy compliance. Review boards represent the next level of governance to assure performance. Committees are constituted as needed to collect information, perform analysis of alternatives, and survey stakeholders so recommendations can be presented to the ESC for consideration and action.

Governance provides the framework, principles, structure, processes and practices to set direction, monitor compliance, and assure performance.

Setting direction assures that stakeholder needs, conditions, and options are evaluated so agreed-on Enterprise objectives can be achieved through disciplined prioritization and decision making. Advisory groups can be formed to study particular problems and formulate recommendations to the ESC. Defining the organizational risk policy is one risk governance function performed by the ESC.

Compliance monitoring is often performed by the Program Management Office (PMO) as part of the Quality Management function; it also assures policy. Compliance monitoring includes metrics management, Service Level Agreement (SLA) reporting, trend analysis, risk modeling, variance analysis, process audits, and root cause analysis (RCA). Enterprise goal alignment is a function of compliance monitoring and includes project management oversight, Enterprise-wide change management oversight, Enterprise-wide issue management, and Enterprise risk management. Risk management is critical to Enterprise goal alignment.

An effective risk management program provides information to Senior Leadership so risks can be treated in a timely manner to minimize the impact to Enterprise goals and objectives. An Enterprise Risk Policy is the most important critical success factor. It must include risk appetite and risk tolerance thresholds. The Enterprise Risk Policy establishes the foundation for the Enterprise Risk Management Plan (E-RMP), the Risk

Review Board (RRB), and Project Risk Management Plans (P-RMP).

P-RMPs establish individual project processes for identifying and reporting project risks. Project risks are submitted to the RRB for consideration to be managed at the Enterprise level.

The E-RMP establishes process for managing Enterprise risks and includes reporting to Senior Leadership.

The RRB performs risk reviews to understand and approve risks, evaluate those risks against the costs required to mitigate them, and direct or approve the risk handling approaches and risk mitigation activities (e.g., Risk Mitigation Plan, Contingency Plan). The goal of the RRB is to assess risks for completeness and consistency, and provide communication of the risks to all stakeholders.

The RRB initially reviews and approves the foundational elements of the risk management program including risk policy, governance structure, risk assessment practices, risk management practices, guidelines, and processes for managing, treating and reporting risks. After approval of the risk management program, the RRB reviews candidate risks on a regular basis (typically monthly) to classify risks, assign risk parameters, approve treatment plans, and continuously evaluate risks.

Governance is about negotiating and deciding amongst different stakeholders' value interests. Consequently, the governance system should consider all stakeholders when making benefit, risk, and resource assessment decisions. For each decision, three questions should be asked: For whom are the benefits? Who bears the risk? What resources are required?

Advisory groups can be formed in addition to committees to consider alternatives for satisfying stakeholder needs, quantifying benefits, assessing risk, etc.

Feedback Loop

An active feedback loop is one area where an organization can derive a tremendous amount of value from risk management. One characteristic of active feedback loops is a defined process that continuously pushes information throughout the organization. Information must be actively and continuously pushed while lessons learned and risk models are developed or modified. Waiting until lessons learned and risk models are "done" is a losing battle. The rapid pace of market changes in today's global economy causes information to become stagnant very quickly. Lessons learned quickly become obsolete if they do not evolve as fast, or faster than, today's dynamic global environment. Actively disseminating information allows project teams to leverage enhanced risk models, lessons learned, and best practices. on a near real-time basis. Wiki, or other collaboration software, are excellent tools for providing active feedback to project teams, especially distributed teams, because it drives active participation in the data collection and dissemination processes.

CHAPTER EIGHT

Establish the Context

Establishing the context under which risks are managed is extremely important. The risk management context essentially establishes the boundaries that the risk management team must operate within and are generally based on parameters established in the risk policy. A vaguely defined or non-existent context causes project teams to flounder and waste limited resources, time, and effort attempting to manage risks that a) they cannot possibly manage or b) may be easy to manage but ultimately will have little to no impact on the final project outcome.

To maximize the effectiveness of project risk management, the context should be confined to the project's budget, schedule, quality, and mission accomplishment. These four context elements are an excellent baseline for all projects and most organizations. As an organization grows or becomes more process mature it can expand the context elements of risk management to encompass other aspects of the organization such as reputation, safety, etc. Confining the risk management context to budget, schedule, quality and mission accomplishment enables the project team to more effectively visualize risks that are most likely to impact the project's outcome and objectives. Being able to visualize risks goes a long way toward the accurate identification of risks and the subsequent treatment of them.

I often encounter organizations that broaden the scope of project risk management to include areas outside of the project team's direct control. Requiring project teams to manage risks well outside of their project boundary not only causes confusion and wasted effort but also indicates the need for a Program / Project Management Office (PMO) or an integrated product team (IPT). PMOs and IPTs are much more capable and effective at managing risks across an organization than a project team.

CHAPTER NINE

Identify Risks

Proper identification of risks is one of the greatest challenges that risk practitioners will face. Project risks frequently have a variety of symptoms, conditions, events, opinions, etc. that indicate the presence of a risk. Project teams often identify risk indicators as the actual risk while the real risk slips by under the radar. The real danger of identifying risk indicators instead of the true risk is that the risk goes undocumented, and undocumented risks simply cannot be managed.

An extraordinarily large risk register is one indication that project risks have not been properly identified. Large risk registers will likely be filled with a combination of risks, risk indicators, issues, opinions, conditions, action items, etc. Large risk registers are not only intimidating but are also simply unmanageable because of their size. Wasted effort and "churning" are byproducts of large risk registers because every risk, condition, symptom, and issue requires significant effort to document, develop treatment plans for, and report the status. This churn leads to project team spending countless hours attempting to manage risk indicators instead of managing the risk that will result in schedule delays, budget overruns, and poor quality. Furthermore, the team's apparent inability to manage their risks leads them to lose confidence in their ability and even calls into question the risk management process itself.

In addition to risk indicators, risk registers frequently contain issues that further compound the problem and lead to even more confusion (e.g. RIO challenges noted above). A risk register containing dozens or hundreds of entries can quickly become daunting and very intimidating to the project team that already questions their ability to effectively manage risks. Case study #2 in Chapter Sixteen illustrates this situation. In that case study, 83% of the risks on the program were not risks as all but conditions, symptoms, opinions, etc.

A hurricane is one example of an event that is often identified as a project risk. There is no question that a hurricane will significantly impact a project team working in a hurricane prone area, but the hurricane itself cannot be managed by the project team. The key point here is to recognize the difference between conditions or events that cannot be managed (e.g. asteroid hitting the earth, hurricanes, earthquakes, etc.) and those risks that can be managed such as schedule delays, budget overruns, and increased defects.

The real risk here is that something (in this case a hurricane) will cause a schedule delay because the project team will be shut down for some number of days depending on the severity of the hurricane. This same risk can be caused by a variety of other events such as a power outage, labor strike, etc. So instead of listing all of the events that could cause a schedule delay, it is easier and much more effective to list a single risk of "schedule delay." The various schedule delays can be effectively managed using triggers and thresholds, which are discussed in more detail in Chapter Twelve.

Risk scenario is an analysis technique presented in Chapter Fourteen to help visualize and understand risks. Risk scenario is a simple structured process designed to clearly articulate risks and their associated impact. The structure of risk scenarios helps sift through conditions, symptoms, events, concerns, and opinions to get to the real risk.

Risks must be defined in terms of schedule impact, budget impact, quality impact, or ability to accomplish the mission. If schedule impact can be effectively managed, then it doesn't matter what condition or event impacts the schedule (i.e. hurricane, network outage, personnel turnover, etc.).

There are five basic questions that can be asked to help identify project risks:

1. Is there a schedule impact?

2. Is there a budget impact?

3. Is there an impact to quality?

4. Is there an impact to our ability to accomplish the mission?

5. Can impact be objectively quantified?

If the answers to questions 1, 2, 3, or 4 and 5 are "yes," then there is a very good chance the risk has been properly identified. Risks should be documented in a manner that clearly articulates the risk and the impact. AS/NZS-4360 suggests that risks be identified using the following construct:

(Something happens) LEADING TO (outcomes expressed in terms of impact on objectives).

Example: A hurricane makes landfall near Tampa, FL LEADING TO a 3 week schedule delay.

An if-then construct can also be used as it is very common and readily accepted in many industries. The if-then construct contains the same components of the AS/NZS recommendation and is widely understood. The "if" clause defines the risk event, the "then" clause establishes the context, and also quantifies the impact to the project.

IF *<risk event>* THEN *<context><impact>*

Example:

IF < hurricane makes landfall near Tampa, FL>
THEN <the schedule>< will be delayed 3 weeks>

The AS/NZS-4360 construct and if-then construct are equally effective in defining risks. I prefer the if-then construct because it is slightly more structured and is widely accepted in Government contracting environments. Regardless, the key point is to define specific risk events and their corresponding, objectively quantified, impact to the project objectives.

Many risk managers believe that risk identification ends when the risk is properly identified and logged in the risk register. However, as stated previously, additional risks may arise as the direct result of managing a risk. It is important to consider the potential for secondary and residual risk when identifying risks and to notate the risk register accordingly. Secondary and residual risks are most often identified when developing risk treatment plans,thereby requiring risk identification to be reconsidered.

To help identify a risk, keep in mind that the impact of the risk must be able to be objectively quantified based on the previously established context (e.g. schedule, budget, quality, and mission accomplishment). Once a risk has been identified it must be added to the risk register. A project risk register should be very simple and easy to maintain. I have seen many risk registers that are extremely complicated spreadsheets that compute everything under the sun and link to different workbooks and spreadsheets. The risk register should be a very simple log that tracks the history of a risk beginning when it is initially identified and continuing through the life of the project or until the risk is fully treated to the point that it no longer impacts the project. Figure 5 is an example of a basic risk register that covers all the bases.

The risk register is intended to provide a summary of the project risks and pointers to other information associated with a given risk. Once again, simplicity is the key to success here. There is little value in collecting volumes of information on risks determined to be acceptable; focus your energy on risks that have the greatest impact to project or organizational objectives. More detailed information about unacceptable risks can be found in the risk treatment plan.

Project Name:			Date Created:	
Project Manager:			Date Updated:	

Risk ID	Risk Event	Context	Impact	Probability	Priority	Secondary Risk ID	Residual Risk ID	Treatment Plan ID	Status

Figure 5 - Risk Register

Risks are identified during the initial project risk assessment but they can also be identified at any point throughout the project life cycle. It is important to add risks to the risk register as soon as they are identified and not wait for a formal risk assessment or brainstorming session. As soon as a risk is identified, some preliminary risk analysis must be conducted to determine whether the impact crosses the threshold of an unacceptable risk. The preliminary analysis should seek to identify the risk context and to objectively quantify the impact.

Figure 6 and Figure 7 are excerpts from an actual risk register that clearly illustrates the importance of properly identifying risks and quantifying their impact. These examples are actual risk statements, although individual and company names have been changed. This particular project used a 5 X 5 prioritization matrix based on the probability and impact tables in Figure 6 and Figure 7. Notice that the Level D and Level E in Figure 6 state the risk cannot be mitigated, and Level A states the risk will be avoided or mitigated through the use of standard practices. According to the probability matrix, the project team need only mitigate risks that fall in Level B and Level C.

PROBABILITY		YOUR APPROACH AND PROCESSES
A	Not Likely	Will effectively avoid or mitigate this risk based on standard practices ~ 10%
B	Somewhat Likely	Have usually mitigated this type of risk with minimal oversight in similar cases ~ 30%
C	Likely	Will mitigate this risk, but workarounds will be required ~ 50%
D	Highly Likely	Cannot mitigate this risk, but a different approach might ~ 70%
E	Near Certainty	Cannot mitigate this risk, no known processes or workarounds are available ~ 90%

Figure 6 - Risk Register Probability Matrix

LEVEL	TECHNICAL PERFORMANCE	SCHEDULE	COST
1	MINIMAL: Minimal or no consequence to technical performance impact	Minimal or no impact	Minimal or no impact
2	SOME: Minor reduction in technical performance or supportability, can be tolerated with little or no impact on program; same approach retained	Additional activities required, able to meet key dates	Budget increase or unit production cost increases
3	MEDIUM: Moderate reduction in technical performance or supportability with limited impact on program objctives; workarounds available	Minor schedule slip, no impact to key milestones	Budget increase or unit production cost increases
4	HIGH: Significant degradation in technical performance or major shortfal in supportability; may jeopardize program success; workarounds may not be available or may have negative consequenses	Program critical path affected, all schedule float associated with key milestones exhausted	Budget increase or unit production cost increases
5	CRITICAL: Severe degradation in technical performance; cannot meet key performance parameter or key technical/supportability threshold; will jeopardize program success; no workarounds available	Cannot meet key program milestones	Exeeds accepted standards/requirements threshold

Figure 7 - Risk Register Impact Matrix

This probability matrix is rather strange in and of itself and we will see how it creates even more problems as the project team starts using it to prioritize risks. The impact matrix in Figure 7 also uses a five level priority scheme, although it uses numbers instead of letters. This impact matrix is fraught with problems, the least of which is that the cost impact for Level 2, Level 3, and Level 4 are the same. How is a stakeholder supposed to interpret the various subjective terms (i.e. minimal, minor, medium, moderate, high, significant, major, critical, etc.)?

Following is a risk statement from the project risk register:

> *Risk 06-1: Generation of the monthly Site/System Usage Report is not possible without the specific details of what metrics are to be reported. Additionally, the software required to capture the data and has not been defined. While Citrix has some capability the Enterprise version is the only one that has the software included. There are many Citrix servers that do not have the required reporting software. The Windows platform does not natively produce the data required. As the exact requirement is defined a Decision Analysis Resolution (DAR) should be completed to assist in the selection of the best product to support the report.*

The first question one must ask is, "What is the risk?" It becomes even more confusing when you add the probability and impact from the risk register. The probability of Risk 06-01 was rated as "Near Certainty" and the impact was "High." The "Near Certainty" rating (Level E, Figure 6) means the risk cannot be mitigated, yet the risk register had a series of mitigating actions.

As an auditor for this project I immediately questioned whether the probability was incorrectly reported or the project was prepared to waste time and effort mitigating a risk that they knew couldn't be mitigated. The impact for this risk was listed as Level 4 (High). Any stakeholder that reviews this risk statement will likely have a series of questions that would include at least

What is the real risk?

What is the real impact?

What is the context?

What is the risk exposure to the Project?

What is the risk exposure to Sponsoring organization?

Risk 06-01 is more of a laundry list of concerns and conditions; there is no risk here.

A second risk statement:

> *Risk 08-01: Lack of access to a defined collaborative environment will impact our ability to standardize processes and tools across the contract in the initial phases. Institutionalization of CMMI practices relies heavily upon our ability to introduce standard toolsets.*

Once again, what is the risk? The probability of Risk 08-01 was rated as "Highly Likely" meaning that the risk cannot be mitigated, and yet again the risk register contained a number of mitigating actions. The impact for this risk was Level 3 (Medium).Once again there is no risk here and this entry should be characterized as a concern.

A third risk statement:

> *Risk 01-05: The current disk storage on the development data-base server is out of date and not supported under the hardware maintenance contract in place. A problem with the disk storage would severely degrade the Project Team's ability to deliver products for an extended period.*

Of the three previous risks, Risk 01-05 is the only risk that could even begin to be stated using the if-then construct. For example: IF <there

is a disk storage outage> THEN <the product delivery schedule><will be delayed ____ months>. The probability for this risk is listed as "Not Likely" but the impact is listed as Level 5 (Critical).

A fourth risk statement:

> *Risk 09-01: Completion of the Customer tasking and Deliverable 06 is contingent on receiving the requirements and CCB direction of resources from the customer. Since we have not yet received these, the task is not on schedule for delivery.*

The probability of Risk 09-01 is listed as "Near Certainty" and the impact is Level 4 (High). Risk 09-01 describes a condition that currently exists and could be an issue, but there is not enough information available to make that determination.

Unfortunately, these entries are typical of what I see when doing project audits where 70% - 80% of the risk register entries are not risks at all. Actual risks in a risk register are frequently so poorly stated it is difficult to understand the degree of impact and the project objectives that will be affected, making it extremely difficult to manage the risk. Using risk scenarios, IF-THEN statements, and 5-questions enable project managers and risk practitioners to properly identify risks as well as quantify the impact to Project or organizational objectives.

CHAPTER TEN

Quantify Risk Impact

To effectively manage a risk, its impact must be objectively quantified. For example, three-week schedule delay, $50,000 budget overrun, 500 hours of rework, etc. Subjective quantification such as "Significant delays," "reduced quality," "Substantial cost overrun," etc. are extremely problematic and must be avoided at all cost. Subjective quantification is very problematic because "substantial cost overrun" to a project manager is entirely different than "substantial cost overrun" is to a CEO.

Quantifiable impact is also crucial when monitoring risks. Risk monitoring must balance the amount of time and effort spent treating a risk with the project impact. It makes little sense to spend $100K to treat a risk that has an impact of $50K. The difficulty in quantifying risk impact is further compounded by the fact that many "risks" are not truly project risks and cannot be managed by the project team; the hurricane scenario previously mentioned is one example. Project teams often struggle to quantify risk impact. Using a risk scenario to decompose the risk into discrete elements makes risk quantification much easier, as illustrated in Chapter Fourteen, Case Study #1.

It is possible that a risk can affect multiple aspects of the project; a schedule delay for example could also impact the budget. To effectively manage the risk it is important to understand the driver(s) behind the project. If time to market is more important, then the risk should be defined and managed as a schedule risk. If budget is more important, then the risk should be defined and managed as a budget risk. The project sponsor will most likely have to make the decision as to whether time to market or budget is most important.

It is possible to manage both a schedule and a budget risk (e.g. project team works unpaid overtime) but often at the risk of quality. The schedule, budget, quality triangle is outside the scope of this text. However, there are countless articles and books available (see links in the Recommended Reading section below). Consider the following scenario based on the "regulatory change" event described in Case Study #1:

- There is a pending regulatory change that will require unplanned modifications to the project

- If the regulatory change goes into effect, then additional scope will need to be added to the project.

Once it has been determined that a risk exists (by asking the five key questions), the next step is to determine the potential impact. In this case, there will definitely be an impact to the schedule, since increased scope will require either additional resources or redeploying existing resources; in either case, the schedule must be modified. In order to determine schedule impact, the scope must be analyzed to some degree and the effort to implement the required changes must be estimated.

Let us assume the scope will require approximately 500 hours of effort to implement; "500 hours" is a quantifiable metric that can be used to prioritize and manage the risk. Based on the project driver(s), the 500-hour estimate can be expressed in terms of schedule impact or budget impact. If budget is the driver, then a part of the treatment plan could be to redeploy existing resources, which would result in a schedule delay but would keep the budget on track. If schedule is the driver, then a part of the treatment plan could be to add additional resources to the project, which would result in cost overrun but keep the original schedule. The schedule impact can be explicitly defined simply by multiplying the number of additional resources required by the duration (e.g. 3 resources redeployed * 4 weeks = 12 week schedule impact). The budget impact can be explicitly defined by multiplying the cost of additional resources times the duration (e.g. 3 additional resources[@ $5,000 / week cost] * 4 weeks = $60,000 budget impact). In this particular scenario, the best approach could be to issue a change order and remove some existing scope in order to accommodate the new regulatory mandated changes. There are other actions that could be implemented, but these serve to illustrate the point.

CHAPTER ELEVEN

Prioritize Risks

After risks have been properly identified and quantified, the next step is to prioritize the risks. Some may argue that developing a risk treatment plan should be the next step in the sequence. But I contend it is more effective to prioritize risks first so that risk management effort can be focused on the high impact risks. It makes little sense to spend time and effort to develop risk treatment plans for low impact risks that will result in schedule impacts of hours or days while the project is on the verge of incurring a risk that will result in schedule delays of weeks or months.

Prioritizing risks before developing treatment plans will yield the most value for the project team by focusing their effort on the high impact risks. Risks should be prioritized based on impact to the project followed by probability or frequency of occurrence. There are countless risk prioritization schemes ranging from very simple high/low schemes to extremely complex schemes such as Monte Carlo simulation.

I strongly prefer ISACA's Risk IT prioritization scheme because it is simple and it rapidly drives people to focus on the most significant risks. As stated in Chapter Five, ISACA's approach is to initially divide risks into two categories of risks: acceptable risks and unacceptable risks. Acceptable risks are contained in the green and blue areas in Figure 8. Acceptable risks are further categorized into acceptable risks (green) and opportunities (blue).

Unacceptable risks are contained in the yellow and red areas. Unacceptable risks are are further categorized into unacceptable risks (yellow) and really unacceptable risks (red).

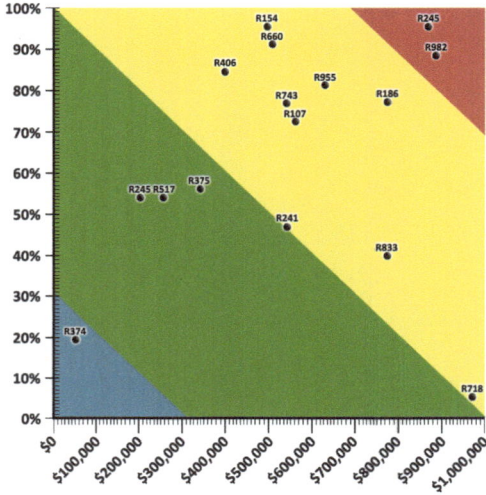

Figure 8 - ISACA Prioritization Matrix

Acknowledging there are acceptable risks enables people and organizations to focus limited resources on the unacceptable risks that will likely have the greatest impact to the project or organization.

Prioritization based on probability of occurrence (depicted by the Y-axis in Figure 8) and impact (depicted by the X-axis in Figure 8) now becomes a relatively simple exercise. One reason I like ISACA's risk prioritization approach is because it clearly portrays the organization's risk tolerance, and everyone can easily see where risks lie in relation to the risk policy and organizational risk tolerance. Another benefit of ISACA's risk prioritization approach is that it can help establish an organization's risk tolerance by plotting acceptable and unacceptable risks on the matrix and adjusting the parameters accordingly.

A further examination of Figure 8 shows that really unacceptable risks are characterized by a probability of impact greater than 65% or an impact greater than $600,000.

Unacceptable risks are characterized by a 100% probability of impact or an impact equal to $1,000,000.

Acceptable risks are characterized by risks that have a probability of impact less than 100% or impact less than $1,000,000.

Finally, opportunities are characterized by probability of impact less than 30% and cost less than $300,000 to implement.

I recognize the ISACA's risk prioritization approach may be too radical of a departure from legacy prioritization schemes that have been around for decades, so we will explore six different prioritizations matrices that are commonly used in many industries.

The risk prioritization matrix shown in Figure 10 is from a U.S.-based professional services firm. It utilizes a 3 X 3 matrix. Risks are prioritized using a basic High, Medium, and Low prioritization scheme. Individual risks are plotted on the matrix based on the impact to the project and probability of occurrence. Treatment plans are developed based on the overall priority. Treatment plans are generally developed for risks that fall in the red-colored boxes.

There are three basic priority groups: red, yellow, and green. The red-yellow-green stoplight paradigm is frequently used throughout many industries to represent risk priorities. The red risks in Figure 9 represent the high priority risks, yellow represents medium prior-

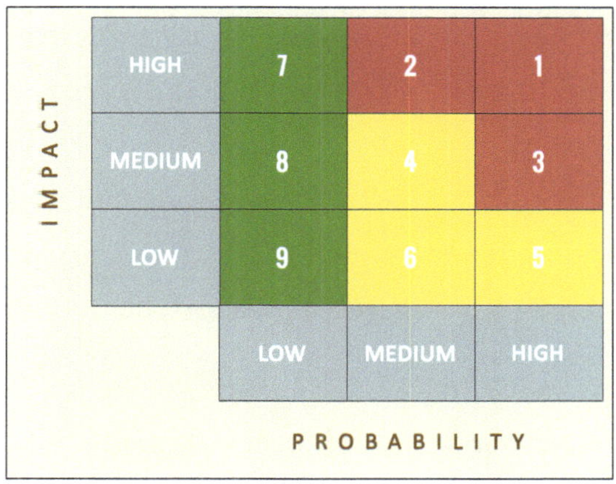

Figure 9 - Professional Services Priority Matrix

ity risks, and green represents low priority risks. High priority risks are further broken down based on their position within boxes 1, 2, and 3. Where box 1 represents the highest of the high priority risks, box 2 represents the next highest priority and so on. Note that impact takes precedence over probability.

Figure 10 - DAU Priority Matrix

Some organizations prefer a larger risk prioritization matrix such as the risk matrix from the Defense Acquisition University (DAU) Risk Management Guidebook shown in Figure 11. The DAU risk matrix utilizes a 5 X 5 matrix and employs the same stoplight paradigm as Figure 10. Like the 3 X 3 matrix, risks are plotted on the risk matrix based on impact and probability. Proponents of a larger prioritization matrix suggest the additional granularity provides more effective prioritization of risks. However, based on my experience, additional granularity often leads to confusion and delays while team members argue about whether a risk should be a 5/5, 4/5, or 5/4. In addition to confusion, large prioritization matrices can lead to resources expending a disproportionate amount of effort on lower priority risks that may have limited impact on the overall success of the project.

I strongly advocate simple prioritization schemes for two reasons. First, complex prioritization schemes are confusing. I have seen risk assessments drag on for days because the team cannot come to consensus on whether a risk should be weighted .1 or .2 in a 10 X 10 matrix. Secondly, there are no industry case studies or research reports that clearly demonstrate more prioritization options improves the effectiveness of risk management.

Objective quantification parameters must be established for high, medium, and low when using these matrix based prioritization schemes. Impact parameters require a quantified value for each context; Table 1 illustrates one example:

CONTEXT	IMPACT	PARAMETER
SCHEDULE	High	> 6 Weeks
SCHEDULE	Medium	2 - 5 Weeks
SCHEDULE	Low	< 2 Weeks
BUDGET	High	> $100,000
BUDGET	Medium	$50,000 - $99,999
BUDGET	Low	< $50,000
QUALITY	High	> 1,000 Hours Rework
QUALITY	Medium	500 - 999 Hours Rework
QUALITY	Low	< 500 Hours Rework
MISSION	High	Failure Chance > 65%
MISSION	Medium	Failure Chance 35% - 65%
MISSION	Low	Failure Chance < 35%

Table 1 - Quantifiable Impact Parameters

The parameters for probability can be the same for all contexts (e.g. schedule, budget, quality, mission accomplishment). I suggest starting with a baseline of >80% for high, 50% - 79% for medium and <50% for low. Over time these parameters can be adjusted based on actual performance in a particular environment.

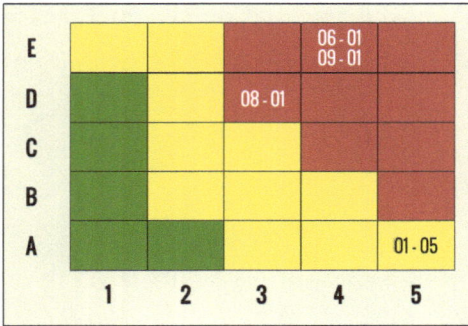

Figure 11 - Risk Matrix

If we refer back to the risk examples presented in Chapter Nine, we see that plotting these four risks on the probability and impact matrix (Figure 11) indicate that 06-01, 09-01, and 08-01 (Red) are critical risks and 01-05 is a moderate risk (Yellow). Recall that Risk 01-05 was the only risk that could be articulated as a risk, yet it has the lowest priority of the four.

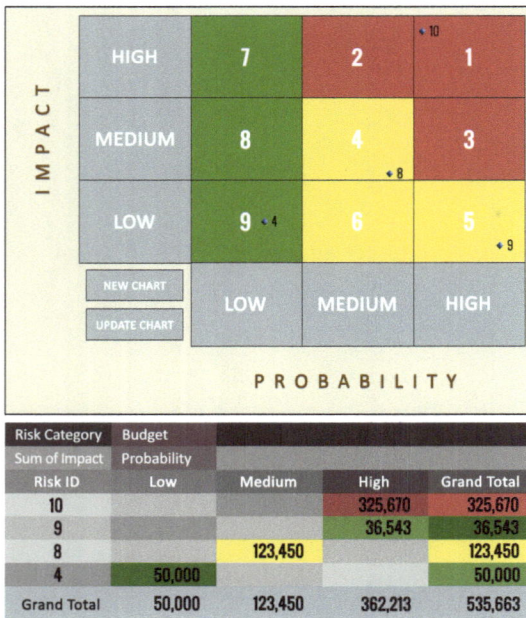

Figure 12 - 9-Box with Risk Exposure

This example clearly illustrates the danger of prioritizing risk using subjective criteria. Subjective criteria can be emotionally charged and lead to protracted discussions because the criteria is easily refuted, thereby wasting valuable time and precious resources. The real danger here is the amount of time and money that will be spent treating and managing the conditions, symptoms, events, or opinions and will likely have no impact on either the outcome or project objectives. In this case, the only real risk has the lowest priority and will likely receive little or no treatment effort, whereas the non-risk items (06-01, 09-01, and 08-01) will receive significantly more attention by virtue of their subjective rating.

A more effective risk prioritization matrix is one that combines probability, impact, and total risk exposure such as the one shown in Figure 12. Concentrating on the impact and probability matrix you will notice there is one high risk (#10), seemingly two moderate level risks (# 8 and #9), and one low level risk (#4). When risk exposure is taken into account the picture changes significantly. First of all, the total risk exposure for this project is $535,663. The top two risks, in terms of risk exposure (#10 and #8), represent 84% of the total risk exposure for this organization. Therefore, spending time and money to treat the 16% associated with the bottom two risks (#4 and #9) does not make good economic sense.

Figure 12 also illustrates how risk exposure plays an important role in risk prioritization. The top two risks (#10 and #8) don't change, but the bottom two risks change based on their degree of budget exposure. Risk #9 only has a budget exposure of $34,543 whereas Risk #4 has a budget exposure of $50,000. This example not only illustrates how prioritizing risks before developing treatment plans prevents wasted effort but also demonstrates the need to understand an organization's risk tolerance. If the organization has a reasonable tolerance for risk, then one can easily make the case to focus all risk management efforts on Risk #10, because that risk alone represents 61% of the total risk exposure. If the organization has a low tolerance for risk, then Risk #10 may represent sufficient risk to warrant avoiding the risk all together. As you can see, risk tolerance, risk appetite, and risk exposure play a critical role in prioritizing risks.

The true impact of a risk is further diluted by normalizing all risks using the Risk Adjusted Cost (RAC) described Chapter Five. The RAC masks the actual risk impact. Using the RAC calculation, a risk with a $225,000 budget impact and a "High" probability of occurrence would have the same adjusted risk cost ($157,500) as a risk with a $175,000 budget impact and a "Very High" probability of impact. Based on the RAC, these two risks are equal. However, there is a $50,000 difference in the estimated impact.

Both ISO 16085 and Risk IT suggest that risk treatment plans include an estimated budget for treating each individual risk. Allocating an appropriate portion of the contingency reserve budget to each risk treatment plan will provide decision makers with more information upon which to make a decision. For example, decision makers can choose to accept the $225,000 risk impact if the cost of treating the risk is less than $50,000 because there is a greater likelihood of the $175,000 risk occurring. Comparatively, if the cost to treat the risk is more than $50,000 the organization will realize a greater return by treating the $225,000 risk and accepting the $175,000.

CHAPTER TWELVE

Treat Risks

The first step in the risk treatment process is to select one of the four industry-accepted risk treatment strategies: avoid, transfer, mitigate, and accept. Risk treatment is one area where I prefer to utilize ISO/IEC 16085 or AS/NZS-4360. Both ISO/IEC 16085 and AS/NZS-4360 have very comprehensive sections related to risk treatment. AS/NZS-4360 contains excellent detailed information about creating treatment plans along with a variety of scenarios to help illustrate the process. The AS/NZS-4360 approach to risk treatment plans is very comprehensive and includes

- Proposed actions

- Resource requirements

- Responsibilities

- Timing

- Performance measures

- Reporting and monitoring requirements.

AS/NZS-4360 includes two components that are notably absent in both the PMBOK and ISO/IEC 16085: "timing" and "performance measures."

The "timing" and "performance measures" can be combined to establish a trigger point for initiating different actions of the risk treatment plan. Having said that, I prefer the ISO/IEC 16085 treatment plans overall because it is very comprehensive and addresses a number of areas that are not covered in either the PMBOK or AS/NZS-4360 (e.g. resource allocation, control measures, environment requirements, treatment change procedures). These missing components are extremely important and contribute to the development of risk models, which are covered later in this text. AS/NZS-4360 utilizes the concept of "triggers," which, when combined with the ISO/IEC 16085 treatment plan, provides an extremely comprehensive and highly effective risk treatment plan.

RISK	RESOURCE REQUIREMENTS	PROPOSED ACTION	TIMING	PERFORMANCE MEASURE(S)	REPORTING & MONITORING
Schedule Delay > 2 weeks due to late delivery by subcontractor	• Contract Specialist • Project Manager	Develop Performance based contract with supplier(s)	Prior to project start		N/A
		Establish weekly milestones	Prior to project start		N/A
		Conduct weekly progress reviews	Weekly - Ongoing		Weekly Progress Report
		Identify alternate supplier(s)	Prior to project start		Project Schedule
		Establish trigger point for engaging alternate supplier(s)	Prior to project start		Project Schedule
		Engage alternate supplier(s)	Earned value <90% at the trigger point OR Earned value <75% at weekly progress review	Earned Value	In accordance with Communication Plan

Figure 13 - Sample Treatment Plan

To help illustrate the use of triggers, consider the following scenario:

- A key deliverable on the critical path has been subcontracted to an organization that has a reputation for late delivery.

- Based on the Treatment Plan in Figure 13, a trigger point has been established and two actions tied to the trigger point (1 – Identify alternate supplier[s] and 2 – Engage alternate supplier[s]).

The key point here is that specific decision(s) or trigger points are explicitly defined along with specific actions that must be undertaken at that point. Explicitly defining actions and the "trigger" to initiate the action reduces the likelihood that actions will slip, and it also makes the treatment plan repeatable. Explicit actions and trigger points are in stark contrast to soft trigger points and subjective criteria (e.g. "engage the alternate supplier when you are sure that the supplier will be late").

Acceptance is the final risk management strategy. There are two categories of risk acceptance: passive acceptance and active acceptance. Passive acceptance essentially means that the project is simply going to accept the risks and deal with the risks as they arise (aka issues). Active acceptance involves establishing a contingency reserve of time, money, and resources to deal with risks as they arise.

> *Passive acceptance is the default risk management strategy for any project or organization that does not have a formal and effective risk management process.*

Acceptance is a reasonable risk management strategy in cases where the cost of mitigating a risk is more than the impact of the risk. Passive acceptance relegates the project or organization to incur nearly all potential risks. Active acceptance is a common strategy when dealing with project or initiatives with many unknowns (e.g. space travel, leading edge development, etc.).

CHAPTER THIRTEEN

Monitor Risk Treatment

There are two categories of risk monitoring: tactical and strategic. Tactical monitoring occurs day to day and is typically conducted by the project team. Tactical monitoring should be conducted on a daily basis and must take performance measures, trigger points, and actual performance into account. The purpose of the tactical day-to-day monitoring is to evaluate whether the risk treatment plan is effectively treating the risk(s). The tactical monitoring process should evaluate actual progress against the performance measures in the treatment plan. Trigger points should be monitored on a daily basis to make sure risk budgets and tolerance levels are not exceeded. It would not be prudent to spend $100K mitigating a risk that will result in $50K loss, so it is very important to measure the cost and effort associated with risk treatments and not blindly execute the risk treatment plan.

Strategic monitoring is conducted as part of management reviews, during internal or external audits, and at the end of projects. Strategic monitoring is forward-looking and focuses on alignment with the organization's risk policy. Strategic monitoring examines risk exposure, tolerance thresholds, and seeks opportunities for long-term process improvement. An important aspect of strategic monitoring is post-project risk analysis. Risk analysis evaluates the results of risk treatment plans and their associated performance measures, looking for patterns and anomalies that become inputs to risk models.

CHAPTER FOURTEEN

Risk Scenarios

Risks, by their very nature, are difficult to visualize because they are some future event that may impact project objectives, and are therefore somewhat intangible. The impression and uncertainty surrounding risks makes them very difficult for people to visualize, document, and manage. Risk scenario is an analysis technique consisting of five components that help people visualize and understand risks, their impact, and actions that will reduce the impact of the risk (ISACA, 2009). Risk scenarios also help to streamline the risk process by consolidating a series of individual risks into a single risk scenario. Developing a comprehensive treatment plan to address a risk scenario will typically address a number of risks, thereby improving the efficiency and effectiveness of the risk management process.

The five components of a risk scenario are: actor, threat type, risk event, assets or resources, and time. The actor is who or what generates the risk. Actors can include internal staff, competitors, regulators, nature, and the market.

Threat type describes the nature of the threat and can include malicious events, accidental events, natural disasters, equipment or process failures, and external requirements.

The event is what causes project or organizational objectives to be impacted. Events can include disclosure (e.g. confidential information), interruption (of services or production capability), theft, destruction, ineffective design, ineffective execution of processes, compliance or regulatory changes, and inappropriate use.

<Actor> GENERATES <Threat> RESULTING IN <Event>
AFFECTING <Asset(s) / Re-source(s)>
LEADING TO <business objective><Impact><Time>

Example: < Government> GENERATES <tax legislation>
RESULTING IN <increased taxes> AFFECTING <small business>
LEADING TO <business growth> <delayed> <12-24 months>

Assets or resources are objects of value that can be affected by the event and lead to impact to project or organizational objectives. Assets and resources include organization, personnel, process assets, infrastructure (e.g. facilities, networks, equipment, communications), and information. There are two dimensions to the time component: duration of the event and timing of when the event occurs. Risk scenarios, like risk statements, can be expressed using a structured context.

Case Study # 1 – Deferred Action

I will use a risk scenario from one of the projects I manage to illustrate how one can develop a risk scenario and how the risk scenario can be used to drive effective risk management. I work as a Federal Contractor for U.S. Government Agency where the project team consisted of approximately 90 people who are responsible for managing gate reviews for all software releases. The team processes approximately 300 software releases each year. Each release has between two and nine gate reviews per release based on the development methodology and complexity of the release.

President Obama signed a memo in 2012 calling for deferred action for childhood arrivals (DACA). DACA applied to certain undocumented young people who came to the U.S. as children and have pursued education or military service here. DACA required several hundred new Government employees to be hired to process the applications and manage the DACA process. DACA directly affected our project team; security clearance processing for new team members was delayed because new Government employees clearance processing took precedence. This resulted in delays of 30-90 days for new team members.

Case Study # 1 – Phase I

The next round of immigration reform is being referred to as comprehensive immigration reform (CIR). CIR is expected to be orders of magnitude larger and more complex than the DACA of 2012. As a project manager for a Government Contractor, the idea of CIR is quite daunting and will undoubtedly have a profound impact on the work being done today as well as in the future. CIR is extremely broad and will affect many different areas of the government. There are so many facets to this risk that it is difficult to know where to start. This is where risk scenarios come into play. The risk scenario process begins by identifying actors, threats, and risk events. The actor in this case is the regulator (e.g. U.S. Government), the threat is an external requirement, and the risk event is regulatory change. Many risk scenarios are not this cut and dried, but actors, threats, and risk events are typically the easiest risk scenario elements to identify.

To identify assets, resources, and time we must first establish the risk scope. Risk scope identification begins by defining the project and/or organizational objectives that will be affected by this risk. Assets and resources are identified once the risk scope is established. Attempting to identify assets and resources before the risk scope is finalized can result in wasted effort, because resources and assets are identified and categorized only, to be discarded later when the risk scope is finalized.

Our organization's inability to comply with CIR will affect our ability to support the customer's mission and will also negatively affect our corporate revenue. It is not uncommon to have risks that affect multiple business objectives. However, stakeholders must agree on a single driver for the risk, otherwise the risk management effort becomes fragmented and eventually deteriorates to the point where risk management efforts are totally ineffective. There are a variety of risk management activities that will protect corporate revenue, but these activities do not necessarily affect the customer's mission risk. Our ability to meet new mission requirements and cope with high volume of changes expected to accompany CIR is driven by our ability to recruit, hire, train, and on-board additional personnel to handle the increased workload. The resource most affected will be the Resource Management team. In addition to identifying the affected resources we have also identified the risk context as mission accomplishment, Step 1 of effective risk management (Establish Context) is now complete.

Security clearance requirements make time the critical risk element in this case. Normal processing duration is 30 – 60 days, but we have observed durations exceeding 180 days in some cases. Clearance processing time gives us the basis for identifying the risk (Step 2 of effective risk management) and quantifying risk impact (Step 3 of effective risk management).

The customer's mission in this case is the ability to implement software updates and enhancements. The risk stated using an IF-THEN construct would be

IF CIR causes clearance processing times to increase,
THEN software releases will be delayed by 3-6 months.

Quantifiable risk impact combined with ISACA's risk prioritization scheme makes risk prioritization quick and easy. Regulatory changes generally must be implemented within 30 days, so a delay of 3-6 months clearly puts this risk in the unacceptable risk category (Step 4 of effective risk management).

Risk scenarios, like risk statements, can be expressed using a structured context. For example:

<U.S. Government> GENERATES <external requirements>
RESULTING IN <regulatory changes>
AFFECTING <resource management team's ability to properly staff the project team>
LEADING TO <software releases><delayed><3 – 6 months>

By virtue of completing a risk scenario we have also completed the first four steps of effective risk management: establish the context, identify the risk, quantify the risk, and prioritize the risk.

The risk scenario is a powerful tool that helps guide project teams and risk practitioners through the risk management process by providing structure and a mechanism to visualize the nebulous nature of risks. It is not unusual to have multiple risk statements and treatment plans associated with a single risk scenario. In Chapter Fifteen we will see the iterative nature of risk management and how risk scenarios can give birth to additional risk statements during the treatment plan development process.

PART III

EFFECTIVE
RISK
MANAGEMENT

CHAPTER FIFTEEN

Risk Treatment Plans

Risk treatment plans are the heart and soul of an effective risk management program. Risk management programs tend to deteriorate rapidly without effective treatment plans. Treatment plans are where the rubber meets the road; they are the mechanism for applying the organization's risk policy. An effective treatment plan will contain background information, governance, treatment actions, and control information.

The background section should include the creation date of the treatment plan along with regular status updates for the actions, scope of the treatment plan, reference documents, glossary or definitions, and governance information such as the change history, issuing authority and approval authority. The issuing and approval authorities should trace back to the risk management plan and risk policy. The scope and reference document section should include risk scenario information.

The treatment actions section should include specific tasks, schedule of activities, resources needed for the tasks, roles and responsibilities, treatment control measures, treatment cost, and environments or infrastructure needed. The roles and responsibilities section should address any coordination among stakeholders or with other team members that must occur for the treatment to be properly implemented. The treatment control measures section should define measures that will be used to evaluate the effectiveness of the risk treatment.

Blindly executing a treatment plan is a common mistake that occurs. The treatment schedule should contain checkpoints to evaluate treatment effectiveness. If the treatment activities are not producing results, it may be more cost effective to change the risk strategy from mitigate to accept and conserve remaining risk management budget. It doesn't make sense to spend $100,000 to mitigate a risk impact of $50,000, so treatment evaluation checkpoints should occur well before the halfway point to assess treatment effectiveness. The organization's risk tolerance must be taken into consideration to determine where in the lifecycle evaluation checkpoints are introduced and how often they are conducted.

Case Study# 1 – Phase II

I would like to expand on the earlier risk scenario case study to illustrate how easy it can be to quickly and easily develop highly effective risk treatment plans. Training and on-boarding new team members are two areas to be affected by the CIR. Training is affected because of the need to quickly train new Government and project team personnel. On-boarding is affected because there could be a gap of several months before resources can be on-boarded. There are two facets to the on-boarding problem: 1) prospective team members get frustrated with the delays and move on to other opportunities and 2) work load significantly increases but we have no cleared personnel to on-board.

To treat the training risk, instructor-led training courses could be converted to computer-based training (CBT) or webinars. Webinars and CBT remove any restrictions from the lack of training rooms and allow nearly unlimited concurrent training sessions. The formal treatment plan for this risk should lay out specific steps and milestones to convert instructor-led training, test the effectiveness of the training, and deploy the new training courses. This particular risk has the added benefit of reducing future training costs regardless of the CIR, and therefore could be categorized as an opportunity.

To treat the on-boarding risk, a ready-pool of cleared resources could be established. The ready-pool concept would require the organization to establish a size threshold for the ready-pool and be prepared to constantly replenish the resource pool as candidates leave the pool. The formal risk treatment plan would include steps, milestones, and checkpoints to source candidates; it would also process security clearance paperwork, monitor the status of security processing, monitor candidate's interest in upcoming opportunities, remove candidates from the ready-pool, and replenish the pools at various intervals.

This process requires a fair amount of work for seemingly little gain if the CIR is never enacted, but this will be time and money well spent if the CIR does come about. Many organizations have a very difficult time coming to terms with the thought of expending time, money and effort with no guaranteed return on the investment, but that is the nature of risk management. Resources are expended in an attempt to reduce the impact of the risk should it occur. Most of us willingly pay home and auto insurance premiums without a second thought because we understand the impact of not doing so. But, we find it very difficult to apply this same thought process to business objectives.

CHAPTER SIXTEEN

CASE STUDIES

Case Study # 2 - Large Government Program

I facilitated a risk assessment on a large Government program that was plagued by delays and overruns. The program was canceled because of delays, cost overruns, and the overall poor quality of the end product. The purpose of the risk assessment was to determine the risks associated with transitioning the legacy software from the system integrator to a third party for maintenance until the system could be replaced. I applied ISACA's Risk IT and risk scenarios to help concentrate the risk assessment effort. This brief case study will focus on the software transition scenario.

Establish Context and Identify Risks

The initial risk assessment identified 35 risks. During the risk analysis phase, risks were restated using an IF-THEN construct and one of three risk contexts (Cost, Schedule, and Mission Accomplishment). Restating risks using IF-THEN statements led the assessment team to see that 29 of the risks (83%) were issues, conditions, symptoms, concerns, or opinions, leaving only six actual risks. The six remaining risks were categorized into three mission risks, two schedule risks, and one cost risk.

A tremendous amount of time and effort would have been wasted if the team continued the risk management process with the original list of 35 risks. Spending extra time to properly identify and quantify risks is a key lesson learned,which is why it is extremely important to properly identify and establish the risk contexts very early in the process. Risk context is one of the most critical aspects of risk management that must be clearly articulated in the risk management plan (RMP). Risk context can vary slightly across business units, so it is more appropriate that risk context be defined in the RMP based on parameters established in the organization's risk policy.

Quantify Risk Impact

Mission risks were quantified based on their impact to operational requirements and the concept of operations (CONOPS) document. Schedule risks were quantified using actual performance data. Cost risks were quantified using actual performance data and validated using independent industry research.

The mission risks include one security risk and two risks that impact key performance parameters. The mission risks are as follows:

IF the code ownership issue is not resolved, THEN critical mission / CONOPS information can be transferred to unauthorized third parties.

IF computational or algorithmic operation problems in the source code are not corrected, THEN requirement #7 will be compromised because system failures will occur.

IF the configuration baselines are not established, THEN requirement #8 will be compromised because software discrepancies exist.

The two schedule risks were quantified using lessons learned and actual effort collected from software change requests. The schedule risks are as follows:

IF dedicated resources are not assigned to transition activities, THEN the transition schedule will slip 20%.

IF software complexity is not resolved, THEN trouble ticket resolution time will increase by 67.5%.

Results from IV&V static code analysis were used to validate software complexity. The static code analysis team had nearly 10 years of experience performing static code analysis on highly complex source code at NASA and Department of Defense (DOD) programs. The static code analysis team was able to process approximately 4.8 static code flags per hour on the NASA and DOD software but was only able to process 1.6 static code flags per hour with the software on this program. The difference between 4.8 and 1.6 code flags per hour represented a 67.5% productivity loss due to code complexity, lack of documentation, inaccurate documentation, and other environmental complexities.

Actual performance data and independent industry research were used to determine the impact for the single budget risk.

IF code analysis flags are not corrected, THEN maintenance costs will increase by $31M.

Actual effort data from change requests was used to calculate the average effort per change request. This actual effort was combined with unreported defects identified during static code analysis. Static code analysis indicated the code base contained approximately 2,229 unreported software defects.

*142.7 hours * 2,229 defects = 318,078.3 hours of effort to correct all of the unreported defects*

A blended billing rate of $95 per hour was used for cost analysis purposes. Multiplying $95 per hour times the 318,078 hours of effort results in a total risk exposure of $30.2 million associated with the unreported software defects. The budget risk exposure seemed extraordinarily high to the assessment team so they used independent industry data to validate the risk exposure. Industry research data from B. Boehm and V. Basili was used to validate the budget risk. Boehm and Basili's research shows the cost of fixing a defect found in Requirements phase is $139, Design phase is $455, Coding phase is $977, Testing phase is $7,136 and Maintenance phase is $14,102 (KPMG, 2009). The software for this program has been deployed and is in the maintenance phase. Multiplying the 2,229 defects by $14,102 equals $31,433,358, which confirms the budget risk ranges between $30 million to $31 million.

Prioritize Risks

At the time this risk was identified, the organization did not have a risk policy, making it very difficult to effectively prioritize the risks. The absence of a risk policy made it extremely difficult to take any risk-related actions because everything was driven based on opinions and individual personalities.

> *A formal risk policy is required to align risk priorities with organizational goals and mission objectives.*

Treat Risks

The stakeholders agreed in principle with the risk but refused to take any action because they felt the impact was unreasonably high. The stakeholder's position on risk impact was quite perplexing given that the impact was based on objective data from two independent sources. The key in cases such as these is to get stakeholders to acknowledge the risk, independent of the impact, and then determine how much they are willing to spend on risk treatment.

It is important to understand that risk treatment does not mean risk elimination; risk treatment is intended to reduce the impact and therefore does not have to be comparable to the impact. In this particular case there was a category of software faults that comprised nearly 40% of the overall faults. The risk assessment team estimated it would cost $4M to correct 40% of the software faults. Spending $4M would reduce the risk exposure from $30.2M to $18M, a ROI of 3:1. Unfortunately, because stakeholders would not acknowledge the risk—because it was seemingly valued too high—they accepted the $30.2M risk exposure by default. This default acceptance is an excellent example of passive acceptance described in Chapter Twelve. In later sections you will see more extreme examples where organizational culture had even greater impact to the organization.

Monitor Risk Treatment

Monitoring risk treatment activities is another critical element for effective risk management. A disciplined approach to risk management is needed in order to avoid overspending on risk management. It doesn't make sense to spend more treating the risk than the result of incurring the risk. Risk monitoring should be conducted on a tactical level by project teams and at an organizational level by some type of oversight organization such as PMO or office of risk management (ORM).

Tactical risk monitoring requires checkpoints and thresholds to be monitored on a daily or weekly basis. Checkpoints are specific, predefined points in the treatment plan where resources expended are compared with the corresponding risk reduction. Expended resources that do not translate to reduced risk should be escalated to the risk review board to determine whether further risk treatment should continue, or if a change in risk strategy is required (e.g. accept, transfer, or avoid). Without predefined checkpoints, project teams tend to expend more time and effort than a risk is worth.

Because the organization did not acknowledge the risk, we have no actual data related to risk monitoring. However, our recommended approach included an iterative development model where we created a series of small releases so we could measure and evaluate the amount of effort required to remove code faults. The expectation was that we could validate the amount of expended resources with the corresponding risk reduction with the first incremental release. There was a checkpoint near the end of each release where we could report to stakeholders and recommend whether to proceed or revert back to accepting the risk. The fact that $4M was allocated to risk treatment did not mean that it should have all been spent if there were indications that the expected risk reduction could not be achieved.

Case Study # 3 – Deepwater Horizon

Deepwater Horizon Overview

There are numerous case studies of the Deepwater Horizon disaster, many of them centering on the sequence of events leading up to and immediately following the well blowout that led to one of the greatest oil spills in history. I find that some of the more interesting research is associated with the organizational characteristics that may likely be the root cause of the catastrophe. I see elements of these organizational characteristics in many of the organizations that I work with. The three organizational characteristics that played major roles in the Deepwater Horizon disaster are undervaluing risk impact, lack of governance and oversight, and schedule and budget pressure.

An analysis of the Deepwater Horizon disaster indicates that British Petroleum (BP) dramatically undervalued the risk of an oil spill from the Macondo well. The Minerals Management Service (MMS), now known as Bureau of Ocean Energy Management, Regulation and Enforcement (BOEMRE), was responsible for approving BP's Oil Spill Response Plan. MMS required oil companies to present their worst case spill scenarios and describe their response plan for those scenarios. BP's Oil Spill Response Plan presented worst case spill scenarios ranging from 28,033 to 250,000 barrels (Davis, 2012). Between 1937 and 2009 there were at least 59 oil spills ranging from 29,000barrels to 6 million barrels. BP's spill scenarios undervalued the spill risk by 1,800% - 16,000%

There is sufficient evidence and testimony to indicate there were significant problems with the goods and services used on the Macondo well project (Bea, 2012). Investigations also indicate numerous failures to properly monitor many aspects of the drilling and capping process. Insufficient and inadequate goods and services combined with the failure of numerous monitoring activities clearly demonstrate a continuous and ongoing lack of governance and oversight; this directly contributed to the well blowout, which resulted in the death of 11 workers and a 5 million barrel oil spill.

The Macondo well project took much longer and cost much more than originally estimated resulting in schedule pressure to complete the well as soon as possible. Evidence indicates there were significant pressures to save time, decrease costs, and develop early production from this very difficult well – the "well from hell" (USCG – BOEM-RE 2010, Committee on Energy & Commerce 2010). These schedule pressures combined with the lack of oversight sowed the seeds of disaster.

The Deepwater Horizon disaster was the result of the simultaneous failure of proactive, interactive, and reactive activities.

Proactive activities are those that are implemented before malfunctions occur (e.g. governance, oversight, quality assurance, quality control).

Interactive activities are those that are implemented after a malfunction occurs. Interactive activities include the ability to properly detect, analyze, and correct failures.

Reactive control measures on the Macondo project included emergency shutdown, blowout preventer, emergency disconnect, containment and mitigation—all of which proved ineffective. Research following the well blowout indicates that had even a single risk barrier not been breached disaster would have been averted.

The Role of Organizational Culture

The dominating factor for the Deepwater Horizon failure is attributed to organizational culture. The lack of QA, QC, and change management early in the project created a cascading scenario in which multiple unabated failures led to the catastrophe. The situation was further compromised by budget and schedule pressure, causing operators and subcontractors to take numerous shortcuts. This resulted in an unrecoverable situation with inadequate and unproven contingency plans and containment procedures.

According to Bea (2011), Carolyn Libuser analyzed five prominent failures: the Chernobyl nuclear plant, Exxon Valdez grounding, Bhopal gas leak, Challenger explosion, and mis-grinding of the Hubble Telescope mirror. The results of Libuser's research indicate Higher Reliability Organizations (HRO) exhibit five organizational characteristics that other organizations do not. HRO have extensive process auditing procedures, reward systems that encourage risk mitigating behavior, quality standards that exceed industry standards, the ability to correctly assess risks, and a strong command and control organization. Successful HRO are preoccupied by failure, reluctant to simplify interpretations, are sensitive to operational situations (e.g. situational awareness), are committed to resilience, and under-specification of structure (Bea, 2012).

The Seeds of Failure

The seeds of failure for Deepwater Horizon were sown long before drilling began. In 2011, members of the Center for Catastrophic Risk Management (CCRM) formed the Deepwater Horizon Study Group (DHSG) to study the disaster to ensure future oil and gas exploration can be conducted in a reliable, responsible, and accountable manner. The DHSG prepared a series of reports detailing the sequence of events, findings, and recommendations. The *Final Report on the Investigation of the Macondo Well Blowout states* "...failures (to contain, control, mitigate, plan, and clean-up) that unfolded and ultimately drove this disaster appear to be deeply rooted in a multi-decade history of organizational malfunctions and shortsightedness." (Deepwater Horizon Study Group, 2011).

According to Bea (n.d.), studies show there are 100+ incidents and 10 to 100 near misses for every accident. Unfortunately, many organizations have neither the risk culture nor robust enough risk governance to recognize these near misses and associate them with risk scenarios that can be managed. Many organizations rely too heavily on tactical risk management and relegate strategic risk management to a check box activity that can be satisfied by having an enterprise risk policy. Effective risk management must include robust strategic activities combined with well-defined tactical risk management activities similar to those activities described in Part II – Elements of Risk Management.

Strategic risk management activities include risk modeling and trend analysis to establish leading indicators based on incidents and near misses. Incidents and near misses will manifest themselves as project issues and operational incidents. Organizations that do not have a risk aware culture often overlook these issues and incidents as risk indicators, because there is no overarching analysis to correlate similar incidents across the enterprise.

CHAPTER SEVENTEEN

TOOLS AND TECHNIQUES

Risk Dashboard

A risk dashboard is associated with the risk register and is one of the most important tools for risk managers and stakeholders. A risk dashboard is a graphical representation of all identified risks. It clearly depicts the greatest risk and where risk management efforts should be concentrated. The dashboard excerpt depicted in Figure 14 illustrates schedule risks plotted on a probability and impact matrix as well as the total risk exposure. Risk dashboards are covered at length in Chapter Eighteen.

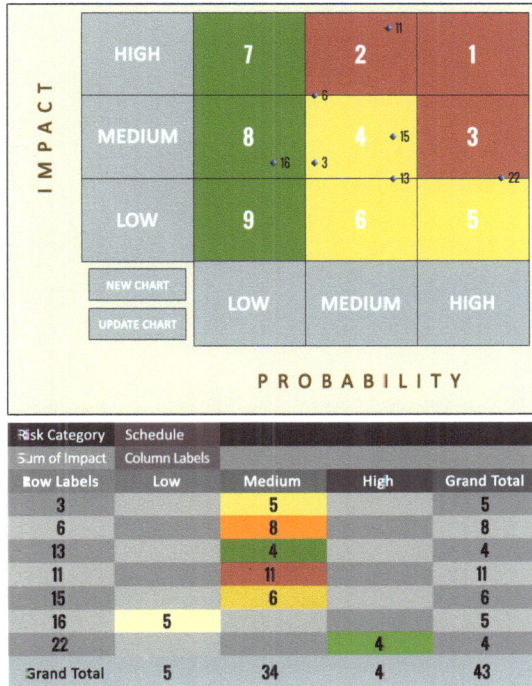

Probability and impact matrix (IMPACT vs PROBABILITY):

	LOW	MEDIUM	HIGH
HIGH	7	2 ← 11	1
MEDIUM	8 ← 16	4 ← 15, ← 3, ← 13	3 ← 22
LOW	9 ← 6	6	5

NEW CHART · UPDATE CHART

Risk Category	Schedule			
Sum of Impact	Column Labels			
Row Labels	Low	Medium	High	Grand Total
3		5		5
6		8		8
13		4		4
11		11		11
15		6		6
16	5			5
22			4	4
Grand Total	5	34	4	43

Figure 14 - Schedule Risk Dashboard

Expected Monetary Value (EMV)

Expected Monetary Value (EMV) is an excellent technique for determining the amount of risk exposure and selecting a course of action based on the amount of risk. EMV is developed using a decision tree. Decision trees consist of decisions that need to be made, decision nodes, and chance nodes. Each node of a decision tree contains one or more decisions that must be made, investments associated with specific decisions, returns that decisions may yield, chances or options, and net path value. Decision trees can be used to determine the most cost effective option to choose, or the option that yields the highest return on investment. Figure 15 shows a simple decision tree used to choose the most cost effective way to travel from Boston to Chicago.

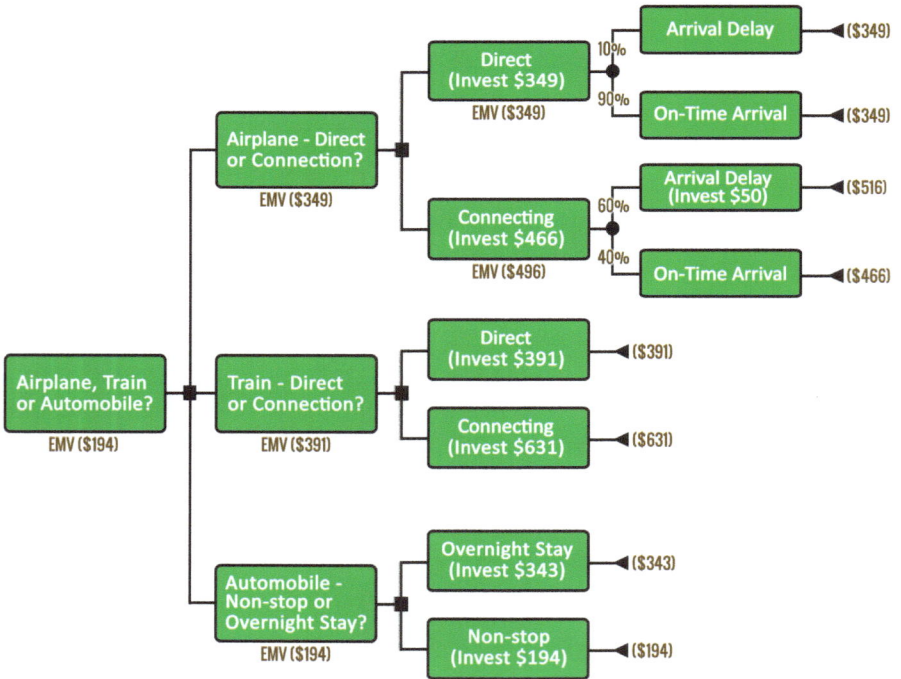

Figure 15 - EMV Chart

Let's start the discussion with a definition of the risk.

IF travel cost exceeds $350 THEN the trip will be canceled.

The decision to be made is which mode of transportation should be used: airplane, train, or automobile. So, this decision tree has three primary nodes, one for each mode of transportation. Each mode of transportation has a different cost; the airplane node has different outcomes based on the probability of delays. Now let's walk through the process of constructing this decision tree.

Decision trees are constructed left to right, but values are computed right to left. To construct the node of a decision tree you must have the decision to be made, the cost associated with the decision, and outcome of the decision. In cases where a single decision has several potential outcomes, one must determine the probability of each outcome. Following the airplane node we see a second decision is needed about whether to take a direct flight or a connecting flight. The direct flight airfare is $349 and the connecting flight airfare is $496.

Keep in mind that we are constructing the decision tree at this point and not computing values so disregard the "EMV $349".

In this example there is a single chance node associated with the direct flight option, where there is a 10% chance that we will arrive late and a 90% chance of arriving on time. The probability of each chance node must equal 100%. There is no limit on the number of chance nodes nor is there a limit on the number of options for each chance node. The connecting flight has a 60% chance of arriving late and also includes an estimated $50 for food and beverages during the layover. There are only two choices on this chance node, so the probability of arriving on time is 40%. The end of the node occurs when there are no remaining decisions or chance nodes.

The net path value is calculated after reaching the end of the node. The net path value (NPV) is the total amount of investments and returns along a path. In this example there are no returns so only investments are computed. The direct flight, late arrival NPV is $349 (initial investment of $349 + $0 additional cost for Arrival Delay). The direct flight, on-time arrival NPV is also $349 (initial investment of $349 + $0 additional cost for on-time arrival). The connecting flight is a different story because additional costs are incurred on the delay node. The connecting flight, arrival delay NPV is $516 (initial investment of $466 + $50 for food and beverage). The connecting flight, on-time arrival NPV is $466 (initial investment of $466 + $0 additional cost for on-time arrival). The construction of the airplane node is complete at this point so we can now compute the EMV.

Construct nodes left to right, compute EMV right to left

Compute the EMV by following each path from right to left, multiplying the probability of each chance node by the outcome of the decision.

Airplane, Direct – ($349 X .1) + ($349 X .9) = $349

Airplane, Connections – ($516 X .6) + ($466 X .4) = $496

The best option is the largest value, in this case ($349).

Similar to the airplane option, there are also direct trains as well as connecting trains. The cost of a direct train ticket is $391 and the cost of a connecting train is $631. The EMV for the train node is $391.

The automobile node also includes two options, a non-stop option and an overnight stay option. The travel cost must be estimated in order to determine the total investment needed. It is 982 miles from Boston to Chicago. The automobile is estimated to average 25 miles per gallon (mpg) and the cost of fuel is $3.80 per gallon. The estimated fuel cost of $149.26 (982 miles / 25 mpg * $3.80 per gallon). The overnight stay option includes an additional $119 for hotel cost and five meals averaging $15 each. The total investment for the overnight stay option is $343 ($149 fuel cost + $119 for hotel cost + $75 for meals). The non-stop option eliminates hotel cost and reduces the meal expense to $45 resulting in a total investment of $194 ($149 fuel cost + $45 for meals). The EMV for the automobile node is $194.

The decision tree is now complete and we have computed EMV for each of the three nodes. Airplane EMV is $349, train EMV is $391, and automobile EMV is $194. We can now evaluate the options that we have. The overall best option is automobile, non-stop because the EMV is $194. The original risk statement indicated the trip would be canceled if the cost exceeded $350. There are two options below $350: airplane with a direct flight is $349 and automobile without an overnight stay is $194.

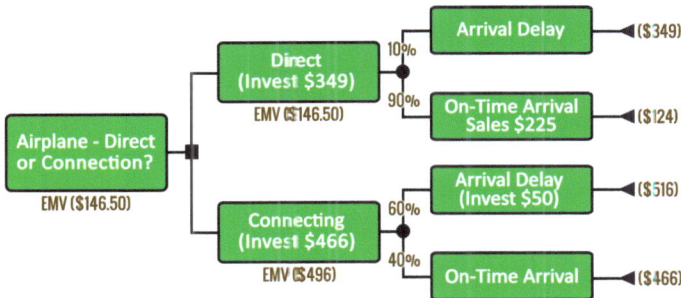

Figure 16 - EMV with Cost and Revenue

If this were a business trip one could make the case that a direct flight with an on-time arrival could offer the opportunity for several hours of sales activity that could generate revenue. To further the discussion, let's assume that an on-time arrival allows us to bill three hours at $75 per hour ($225 in revenue). Figure 16 shows how the EMV changes with the added revenue. The $225 in sales increases the NPV from $349 to $124. Recalculating the airplane EMV yields $146.50, which is now $48 less than driving non-stop. The key point of this exercise is that decision trees drive people and organizations to make fact-based decisions using objective data instead of making decisions based on generalized or subjective data. Objective data allows us to counter the statement, "It's cheaper to drive than it is to fly" with, "Yes it is $155 cheaper to drive than to fly, but flying allows us to generate $225 in additional revenue, which makes flying more cost effective by $48."

Risk Models

One of the most important outcomes of the risk analysis process is the development of risk models. A risk model is a risk strategy, risk scenario or risk treatment plan that has been proven to be effective for a recurring risk. A risk model will contain proven mitigating strategies, resources, proposed actions, triggers, performance measures, and reporting information. Additionally, the risk model will include risk strategies and/or treatments that were applied but were found to be ineffective.

Risk models can be developed based on a variety of factors (e.g. methodology, project size, team size, technology stack). The real value of the risk model is that effective actions and strategies are validated and ineffective actions are documented so that subsequent project teams can focus on proven treatment plans. Maintaining risk models based on risk scenarios is an effective technique that yields significant value to the organization and assures alignment with business objectives as they evolve with the constantly changing marketplace.

CHAPTER EIGHTEEN

Risk Management Maturity

Like other maturity models, risk management maturity is characterized by organizations moving from chaotic, ad hoc process environments to well defined, efficient, and highly effective process environments. Risk management maturity consists of four basic levels

> **Level 1** – Ad hoc processes that are inconsistently applied across the organization;
>
> **Level 2** – Well defined risk management processes that are generally applied across the organization;
>
> **Level 3** – Risk governance guides risk management practices and organizational focus on risk management effectiveness metrics;
>
> **Level 4** – Fully institutionalized risk management processes, procedures, and metrics that demonstrate the organization's ability to effectively manage risk and quantifiably demonstrate risk reduction.

Aligning with the PMBOK provides a minimal level of risk management maturity, and is characterized by well-defined processes that are consistently applied across the organization. This level of risk management maturity enables organizations to implement efficient risk management practices but limits their ability to objectively quantify risk reduction. A

PMBOK-based risk management approach enables organizations to implement leading indicators such as INCOSE's risk treatment leading indicator. The steps needed to implement risk treatment as a SE leading indicator are listed in Section 4.0.

Leveraging other industry standards such as ISO 16085, ISO 31000, and COBIT typically yields a much higher level of risk management maturity. This higher level of risk management maturity is characterized by objective risk metrics that clearly demonstrate an organization's ability to reduce their risk exposure. A mature standards-based risk management approach also sets the stage for an organization to leverage additional risk leading indicators, such as INCOSE's risk exposure trends.

1. The risk management roadmap described herein consists of the seven elements

2. Entry criteria required to enter each level of risk management maturity

3. Characteristics that an organization should exhibit for each level of maturity

4. Key processes, tools, etc. that will help improve the risk management maturity of the organization and facilitate movement to a higher level of maturity

5. Steps required to use risk treatment as a leading indicator to evaluate the effectiveness of managing risks

6. Candidate metrics for measuring risk management maturity

7. Suggested audit and oversight activities that will help move the organization through the various maturity levels

8. Exit criteria for moving from one level of maturity to the next

Risk Management Maturity Roadmap

The roadmap to risk management maturity requires process discipline and management commitment. Process discipline starts with the development of processes, procedures, and the development of tools and techniques. Management commitment is required to propagate the risk management process and procedures throughout the organization and support the oversight required to mature the risk management processes and governance.

Level 1 – Ad hoc Risk Management

Acknowledgment by Senior Management that risk management should be practiced is the initial and most important entry criteria for Level 1. The second entry criteria is that risk management process owners are identified and have the authority to define and implement risk management processes.

There are seven characteristics that define Level 1 risk management organizations.

1. Risk management processes may or may not be formally defined and risk management practices are inconsistently applied across the organization.

2. No formal risk management process assets exist. Risk registers are used but formats, processes, methods, etc. differ from project to project.

3. Risk management activities are performed but risks are regularly incurred.

4. The organization does not define risk budgets for either impact or for risk management activities.

5. Risk registers are used on most projects but they contain conditions, symptoms, events, issues, concerns, and opinions. Risks are not clearly articulated and are often confused with issues.

6. Risk mitigation is the predominant risk treatment strategy.

7. No formal risk management training is provided. Organizations must rely on individual's experience and willingness to secure training from outside of the organization.

Key tools, techniques, and processes that help mature the organization's risk management maturity include:

• Tools - risk registers, risk management tools, risk management plan (RMP) templates

• Techniques - facilitated risk assessments

• Processes - formal risk management training, technical certifications (e.g. PMI RMP, ISACA CRISC)

The percentage of properly identified risks versus non-risks in risk registers is one of the most important metrics for maturing risk management. It is nearly impossible for an organization to progress past Level 2 unless risks are properly defined and quantified. Improperly identified risks result in countless hours of wasted effort and wasted budget dollars as time and effort is expended on conditions, symptoms, concerns, and issues while the actual risk becomes imminent.

The percentage of projects that comply with the defined risk management processes is another metric that will help mature risk management. Understanding the extent that risk management processes are implemented allows Senior Management to provide additional guidance and support to expand the implementation of risk management best practices.

Level 1 organizations should follow a dual-pronged approach consisting of high-level audits that touch all projects and a limited number of "deep dive" audits that will provide detailed insight on a limited number of projects.

High-level audits should be used to gauge the degree to which risk management processes are institutionalized across the organization. These audits can also evaluate whether organizational risk management processes assets are being utilized, and can identify improvement opportunities for organizational tools, techniques, and processes.

Conduct a high-level audit of organizational processes and procedures in order to determine the baseline risk management maturity of the organization.

Conduct deep dive audits using a sampling approach that provides access to a diverse cross section of the organizations projects (e.g. large, small, limited risk management, extensive risk management). A main focus of the deep dive audits is to determine the percentage of risks that are properly identified by examining risk registers, issue logs, the results of risk assessment sessions, and risk treatment plans. The results of these audits will be used to improve the quality of risk identification so that effective treatment plans can be developed and the organization can elevate its risk management maturity level.

Consistent risk management practices that are applied across the organization and properly identified risks are the two primary exit criteria from Level 1. Organizations that consistently apply defined risk management practices throughout their entire organization and have eliminated issues, concerns, and risk symptoms from their risk registers are well positioned to elevate their risk management maturity to Level 2 and beyond. These two exit criteria should be based on objective results from the audits referenced in Section 2.1.5.

Level 2 – Defined Risk Management

Organizations that achieve Level 2 can begin to take advantage of the INCOSE risk treatment leading indicator. Risk treatment actions are the basis for measuring risk treatment trends. There are eight characteristics that define Level 2 risk management organizations.

1. The organization has a formally defined risk management pro-

cesses including RMPs.

2. RMPs are consistent across the organization and comply with the defined risk management processes. RMPs are appropriately applied to all projects and initiatives and are in accordance with tailoring and waiver guidelines.

3. Risk registers contain well defined risks (i.e. no conditions, no symptoms, no issues, etc.) using industry accepted risk definition language such as IF-THEN constructs.

4. Risk management processes support a variety of risk treatment strategies that are applied across the organization. Risk registers include all risks, even those that are accepted, avoided, and transferred.

5. Accepted risks are formally tracked.

6. Risk budgets are defined for treatment activities.

7. Efficiency metrics are collected and reported.

8. Risk impact is based on qualitative data.

Key tools, techniques, and processes that will help mature the organization's risk management maturity include:

- Tools – risk treatment plan templates

- Techniques – trend analysis

- Processes – risk identification, impact estimation based on probability or frequency

Organizations that reach this level of risk management maturity will see that risk management processes are fully institutionalized across the organization, and risk models will begin to emerge from trend analysis results.

Level 3 – Governance Guides Risk Management

Organizations that achieve Level 3 of risk management maturity are poised to take advantage of risk exposure as a leading indicator. Risk exposure trend analysis objectively demonstrates an organization's ability to reduce their Enterprise risk exposure. Senior Management of Level 3 organizations recognize that organizational risk policy must address risk tolerance and risk appetite, while tracking to organizational goals and objectives. There are seven characteristics that define Level 3 risk management organizations.

1. Risk policy that includes risk appetite, risk tolerance, and corresponding thresholds.

2. RMPs are consistently applied across the entire organization.

3. RMPs include procedures for establishing and using risk management budgets.

4. Risk exposure is a key performance metric.

5. Emphasis on effectiveness metrics versus efficiency metrics.

6. Effectiveness metrics related to risk treatment planning and risk reduction are established.

7. Improvement initiatives are based on risk exposure and effectiveness metrics.

8. Recognize frequency is a viable alternative to probability.

Key tools, techniques, and processes that will help mature the organization's risk management processes include:

- Tools - risk registers, risk management tools, RMP templates

- Techniques - facilitated risk assessments

- Processes - formal risk management training, technical certifications (e.g. PMI RMP, ISACA CRISC)

Organizations that reach this level of risk management maturity will recognize that risk budgets must be established and risk treatment activities must be tracked against budgets.

Level 4 – Demonstrated Risk Reduction

Organizations that achieve Level 4 of risk management maturity utilize a standards-based approach (e.g. PMBOK, ISO, and COBIT). There are four characteristics that define Level 4 risk management organizations.

1. Risk management policy is well understood by all stakeholders.

2. Organizational discipline to monitor but not necessarily treat acceptable risks.

3. Fully institutionalized risk management process that results in highly effective risk identification, objective quantification of risk impact, and disciplined prioritization.

4. Demonstrated ability to reduce risk exposure.

Key tools, techniques, and processes that will help mature the organization's risk management maturity include:

- Tools - risk registers, risk management tools, RMP templates

- Techniques - facilitated risk assessments

- Processes - formal risk management training, technical certifications (e.g. PMI RMP, ISACA, and CRISC)

RISK MANAGEMENT MATURITY MATRIX
Risk Management Characteristics

	Risk Management Characteristics	YES	NO
LEVEL 1	Risk management practices are inconsistently applied across the organization		
	Risk registers are used but formats, processes, methods, etc. differ from project to project		
	Risks are regularly incurred		
	Risk budgets are NOT defined		
	Risk registers contain conditions, symptoms, events, issues, concerns, and opinions		
	Risk management training is provided		
	Risk mitigation is the predominant risk treatment strategy		
LEVEL 2	Formally defined risk management processes		
	Risk management plan(s) used on most projects or initiatives		
	Risk management plan(s) are consistent across the organization		
	Risk registers contain well defined risks (i.e. no issues, etc.)		
	Variety of risk treatment strategies are applied across the organization		
	Impact is measured using qualitative data		
	Accepted risks are formally tracked		
	Recognition that risk budgets must be defined		
	Efficiency metrics are collected and reported		
LEVEL 3	Risk policy that includes risk appetite, risk tolerance, and corresponding thresholds		
	Risk management plans are consistently applied across the entire organization		
	Impact is measured using quantitative data		
	Risk exposure is a key performance metric		
	Emphasis on effectiveness metrics versus efficiency metrics		
	Improvement initiatives are based on risk exposure and effectiveness metrics		
	Recognition that frequency is a viable alternative to probability		
LEVEL 4	Standards-based approach (e.g. PMBOK, ISO, COBIT)		
	Risk management policy is well understood by all stakeholders		
	Organizational discipline to monitor (and not treat) acceptable risks		
	Fully institutionalized risk management process that results in effective risk identification and objective quantification of risk impact		
	Demonstrated ability to reduce risk exposure		

Figure 17 - Risk Management Maturity Checklist

CHAPTER NINETEEN

AN IMPLEMENTATION STRATEGY

Conclusion

Unfortunately, there is no single, definitive source for risk management processes, tools, techniques, etc. However, highly effective and comprehensive risk management process can be constructed using components of the PMBOK, AS/NZS-4360, and ISO/IEC 16085. The PMBOK contains a good overview of project risk management and includes what should be considered the basic foundation for the strategic aspects of organizational risk management (e.g. risk models, risk management oversight, quantitative risk analysis). ISO/IEC 16085 has a very comprehensive risk management plan, an excellent approach to risk treatment, and also includes more detailed governance topics (e.g. risk management policies, risk management roles and responsibilities, risk thresholds). Even though AS/NZS-4360 has been superseded by ISO/IEC 16085 it does contain more detailed processes along with a number of tools and techniques that can be used to augment ISO/IEC 16085. Additionally, AS/NZS-4360 utilizes the concept of triggers, which simplifies the decision making process in times of crisis and yields repeatable risk treatment plans.

Finally, keep in mind that risk management is not a complex process. The key to effective risk management is to follow a defined, disciplined approach and focus on objective measures for identifying, quantifying, and prioritizing risks. Keep in mind the eight principles of Taoism: disciplined, focused, sensitivity, simplicity, cultivated, independence, joyous, and flexibility. Table 2 shows the relationship between the Taoist principles and characteristics of effective risk management.

PRINCIPLE	RISK MANAGEMENT CHARACTERISTIC
Disciplined	A defined process has been implemented
Focused	Risks are properly identified
Focused	Risks are prioritize based on probability and impact
Focused	A treatment strategy is selected for all risks
Focused	Treatment plans are continuously monitored
Sensitivity	Risk impact is quantified using objective measures
Simplicity	Treatment plans for top risk only
Cultivated	Reusable risk models are developed
Independence	Independent oversight is applied to assure compliance
Joyous	An active feedback loop is institutionalized
Flexibility	Use risk models and active feedback to quickly adapt to the ever-changing environment

Table 2 - Taoist principles and characteristics of effective risk management

Risk Management Implementation Plan

Implement a defined process by developing a risk policy that includes governance, tolerance, roles and responsibilities, and forward references where risk management processes are located. Risk management processes should be contained in one or more Risk Management Plans (RMP). Large organizations may have multiple levels of RMPs beginning with an Enterprise Risk Management Plan (ERMP) and ending with a Project Risk Management Plan (RMP). RMPs describe how risks are identified, quantified, prioritized, managed, and treated. Governance includes risk review boards and their relationship with overall Enterprise Governance (e.g. Steering Committees, Architecture Review Board (ARB), Change Control Board (CCB), etc.). Governance also includes risk thresholds and tolerance levels. Roles and Responsibilities defines specific roles within the organization and what responsibilities they have in the risk management process.

Establishing a baseline of risk management maturity is the next step. A baseline is needed to demonstrate progress so the organization can see improvement. Basic measures that can be used to establish a preliminary baseline include:

- Number of projects/portfolios/programs that have a RMP.

- Number of projects/portfolios/programs that are performing risk management in accordance with their own RMP.

- Number of projects/portfolios/programs that are performing risk management without a documented RMP.

- Number of projects/portfolios/programs that have a RMP that complies with established standards (e.g. SELC, PMBOK, ISO/IEC 16085).

- Number of properly documented risks (e.g. IF risk event THEN consequence).

- Number or percentage of properly documented risk treatment plans.

These preliminary baseline metrics can be collected by conduct process audits. Process audits will identify the existence or absence of RMPs and standards compliance. Program or project reviews can be used to determine the quality of risk statements. Risk treatment plan assessments can help determine the quality and effectiveness of risk treatment plans.

The next step is to identify projects/programs/portfolios that have high quality risk registers and corresponding treatment plans that can be showcased as models for others to adopt. Showcasing existing projects can help establish a grass roots movement that can rapidly speed adoption of best practices.

The early stages of risk management maturity require patience and perseverance. The key is to keep the process moving but not overwhelm the organization by forcing too much change too fast. A sampling methodology for conducting "deep dive" assessments is better in the early stages of maturity than an aggressive comprehensive risk audit process.

Organizations that reach this point will have achieved a basic level of risk management maturity. The emphasis up to this point has been the disciplined and focused Taoist principles that are driven by risk policy and RMPs. The implementation and adoption of a risk policy and RMPs yields the basic process infrastructure needed to sustain effective risk management. To mature beyond basic risk management, organizations must change their focus from process implementation to process improvement. Process improvement requires organizations to focus on the remaining six Taoist principles of sensitivity, simplicity, cultivated, independence, and flexibility resulting in joyous celebration. Adopting a formal process model (e.g. CMMI, ISO, ITIL, SixSigma) will provide the process improvement roadmap that will yield the risk management characteristics shown in Table 2.

Recommended Reading

There are a number of excellent risk management books and papers that provide insight into effective risk management. Following are books, papers, and articles I find most useful and interesting:

Davis, M. (2012). Lessons Unlearned: The Legal and Policy Legacy of the BP Deepwater Horizon Spill. *Washington and Lee Journal of Energy, Climate, and the Environment*, *3*(2), 155-170.

http://law.wlu.edu/dep-images/journal%20of%20energy,%20climate,%20and%20the%20environment/3-2-6-Davis.pdf

Sutcliffe, K. M. (2011, June). High reliability organizations (HROs). *Best Practice & Research Clinical Anaesthesiology*, *25*(2), 133-144.

http://www.clinicalanaesthesiology.com/action/doSearch?journalCode=ybean&occurrences=all&searchScope=fullSite&searchText=hro&searchType=quick&authfield=Sutcliffe%2C+Kathleen+M.%2C+PhD&filterModify=true

Taleb, N. (2007, April 22). The Black Swan: The Impact of the Highly Improbable. *The New York Times*. Retrieved from

http://www.nytimes.com/2007/04/22/books/chapters/0422-1st-tale.html?_r=1&ex=1178769600&en=bdae1078f-2b4a98c&ei=5070

Douglas W. Hubbard entitled *The Failure of Risk Management, Why it's Broken and How to Fix It.*

http://www.hubbardresearch.com/publications/the-failure-of-risk-management-book/

Bibliography

Answers.com. (n.d.). *Unknown Unknowns*. Retrieved from http://www.answers.com/topic/unknown-unknown

Bea, R. G. (2011, January). Risk Assessment and Management: Challenges of the Macondo Well Blowout Disaster. *Deepwater Horizon Study Group*, (5-35).

Bea, R. (n.d.). *APPROACHES TO ACHIEVE ADEQUATE QUALITY AND RELIABILITY*. Berkely, CA: Center for Catastrophic Risk Management.

Boehm, B., & Basili, V. (2001, January). Software Defect Reduction Top 10 List. *Software Management*, (), 135-137.

Davis, M. (2012). Lessons Unlearned: The Legal and Policy Legacy of the BP Deepwater Horizon Spill. *Washington and Lee Journal of Energy, Climate, and the Environment*, *3*(2), 155-170.

Deepwater Horizon Study Group. (2011). *Final Report on the Investigation of the Macondo Well Blowout*. Berkley, CA: Deepwater Horizon Study Group.

Defense Acquisition University, (2006). *Risk Management Guide for DoD Acquisition* (Sixth Edition, Version 1.0). Fort Belvoir VA: Defense Acquisition University. Retrieved from http://www.dau.mil/pubscats/PubsCats/RMG%206Ed%20Aug06.pdf

Halley, M.E. (1693). *An Estimate of the Degrees of the Mortality of Mankind, Drawn from Curious Tables of the Births and Funerals at the City of Breslaw; With an Attempt to Ascertain the Price of Annuities upon Lives*. Philosophical Transactions of the Royal Society of London , (), 596-610 .

Hubbard, D. W. (2009). *The Failure of Risk Management: Why It's Broken and How to Fix It*. Hoboken, New Jersey: John Wiley & Sons, Inc..

Information Systems Audit and Control Association (ISACA). (2009). *The Risk IT Practitioner Guide*. Rolling Meadows, IL: Information Systems and Control Association (ISACA).

Joint Standards Australia/Standards New Zealand Committee OB-007, (2004). *Risk Management* (3rd ed.). Sydney, Australia: Standards Australia International Ltd.

Joint Technical Committee ISO/IEC JTC 1, Information technology, Subcommittee SC 7, Software and system engineering, (2006). *Systems and software engineering — Life cycle processes — Risk management* (2nd ed.). Geneva, Switzerland: International Organization for Standardization/International Electrotechnical Commission.

KPMG. (2009). *Government IT Projects Need QA/IV&V*. : KPMG.

Leung, M. (n.d.). *Chronology of Probabilists and Statisticians* . University of Texas El Paso. Retrieved from http://www.math.utep.edu/Faculty/mleung/probabilityandstatistics/chronology.htm

Libuser, C. B. (1994). *Organizational structure and risk mitigation.* (Order No. 9427348, University of California, Los Angeles). *ProQuest Dissertations and Theses,* , 218-218 p. Retrieved from http://search.proquest.com/docview/304083303?accountid=458. (304083303).

Lustgarten, A. (2010, April). Chemicals Meant To Break Up BP Oil Spill Present New Environmental Concerns. *ProPUBLICA,* (), . Retrieved from http://www.propublica.org/article/bp-gulf-oil-spill-dispersants-0430

Martin, P. K. (2005). "Auditing the Risk Response Plan". Sponsoring a Project. Martin Training Associates. Books24x7. <http://common.books24x7.com/book/id_12615/book.asp> (accessed March 7, 2010)

Ming-Dao, D. (1996). *Everyday Tao: living in balance and harmony*. New York, NY: HarperCollins Publishers.

Project Management Institute, (2008). *A Guide to the Project Management Body of Knowledge* (4th ed.). Newtown Square, PA: Project Management Institute, Inc.

Risk. (n.d.). In *Merriam-Webster OnLine Search*. Retrieved from http://www.merriam-webster.com/dictionary/risk

Sokolnikoff, L.S., & Sokolnikoff, E.S. (1941). *Higher Mathematics for Engineers and Physicists* (2nd ed.). New York and London: McGraw-Hill Book Company, Inc.

Sullivan, J., & Beach, R. (2009, February). Improving project outcomes through operational reliability: A conceptual model. *International Journal of Project Management*, (27), 765-775.

Sutcliffe, K. M. (2011). High Reliability Organizations (HROs). *Best Practice & Research Clinical Anaesthesiology*, *25*(2), 133-144.

Taleb, N. (2007, April 22). The Black Swan: The Impact of the Highly Improbable. *The New York Times*. Retrieved from http://www.nytimes.com/2007/04/22/books/chapters/0422-1st-tale.html?_r=1&ex=1178769600&en=bdae1078f2b4a98c&ei=5070

Wideman, R. M. (1992). Project & Risk Management A Guide to Managing Project Risks & Opportunities. Newtown Square, PA: Project Management Institute, Inc.

Index